THOMAS AQUINAS
AND RADICAL ARISTOTELIANISM

THOMAS AQUINAS
AND RADICAL ARISTOTELIANISM

by

Fernand Van Steenberghen

THE CATHOLIC UNIVERSITY OF AMERICA PRESS
WASHINGTON, D.C.

B
765
.T54
57L

Library of Congress Cataloging in Publication Data

Steenberghen, Fernand van, 1904-
Thomas Aquinas and radical Aristotelianism.

Revisions of three lectures given at Catholic University of America in March 1978.
Includes bibliographical references.
CONTENTS: Introduction.—The first lecture, Eternity of the world.—The second lecture, Monopsychism.—The third lecture, Rationalism. 1. Thomas Aquinas, Saint, 1225?-1274—Addresses, essays, lectures. 2. Aristoteles—Influence—Addresses, essays, lectures. I. Title.
B765.T54S72   189'.4   80-10137
ISBN 0-8132-0552-2

TABLE OF CONTENTS

INTRODUCTION

One of the more fascinating chapters in the history of medieval philosophical thought centers around the intellectual crisis that occurred at the University of Paris in the 1260's and 1270's. Sometimes referred to as "Latin Averroism" and sometimes as "Heterodox" or "Radical" Aristotelianism, a philosophical movement then developed in the Faculty of Arts at the University which was destined to have widespread repercussions on the intellectual life of the period, and which would soon encounter ecclesiastical censure by Stephen Tempier, the Bishop of Paris, in 1270 and especially in his sweeping Condemnation of 1277. Of particular interest to historians of philosophy are the positions developed by leading members of this radical group, especially by Siger of Brabant and Boetius of Dacia. Equally interesting are the philosophical and doctrinal responses to the same by other leading thinkers of that time, most notably, St. Bonaventure and St. Thomas Aquinas.

Great strides have been made by recent and contemporary scholars concerning our knowledge of the teachings and the careers of these radical Masters from the Arts Faculty. Essential to this progress has been the discovery, identification, and edition of many works authored by Siger, Boetius and other Masters in Arts from that period. Long recognized as an authority on thirteenth-century philosophy in general and on Siger of Brabant and Thomas Aquinas in particular, Canon Fernand Van Steenberghen of the University of Louvain has recently drawn upon decades of personal research in this area as well as the latest findings by others throughout the scholarly world in order to produce in 1966 a truly classical general interpretation of that time, *La philosophie au XIIIe siècle.*

Among the recent advances in our knowledge of Siger of Brabant has been the discovery and subsequent edition of his previously unknown Commentary on the *Liber de causis* (A. Marlasca, *Les Quaestiones super Librum de causis de Siger de Brabant*, Louvain-Paris, 1974). Recovery of this work has been especially satisfying to Professor Van Steenberghen because it confirms in striking fashion his long debated contention that there was a shift in the later Siger's thinking in a more orthodox direction. Critical editions of this treatise as well as of most of Siger's important works have now appeared in the important series of studies and texts founded by Professor Van Steenberghen himself, *Philosophes médiévaux.* Consequently, in 1977 he completed and published what must now be recognized as the most definitive work yet written on Siger, his *Maître Siger de Brabant.* In March, 1978, The Catholic University of America invited Professor Van Steenberghen to its campus in order to confer upon him an honorary doctorate. During his stay here, he delivered three lectures which build upon and summarize much of the most recent research concerning the encounter between Thomas Aquinas and the radical Aristotelians, especially Siger of Brabant. Faculty members from the University's School of Philosophy then asked him to expand upon these lectures and to prepare them for publication. This he has now done.

As he himself indicates, he has chosen the path of

doctrinal history in order to develop his theme, Aquinas' reaction to radical or heterodox Aristotelianism. In each of his Lectures he has singled out one central and contested point: in the first, the problem of the world's eternity; in the second, monopsychism, or the view according to which there is only one intellect for all mankind; and in the third, the issue of rationalism.

Himself always the philosopher as well as the historian of philosophy, Professor Van Steenberghen has complemented his historical presentations of these themes with interesting and challenging critical comments. Thus while his general sympathy for the philosophical thought of Thomas Aquinas is widely known, this does not prevent him from going his own way whenever his personal philosophical judgments differ from those of the great Dominican Master. The reader will not be too surprised, therefore, to find Professor Van Steenberghen siding with Bonaventure rather than with Thomas in the controversy concerning the possibility of demonstrating that the world began to be. And if his contention that pre-Thomistic Christian anthropology was spiritualistic and dualistic is not unexpected, his complaint that the *language* in which Aquinas expresses his own anthropology is also dualistic may startle some readers. While his refusal to credit any of the Radical Aristotelians of the 1260's and 1270's with the notorious "double-truth" theory is in accord with the views shared by most serious historians of medieval philosophy today, his detailed examination of this oft-misapplied and misunderstood expression should prove rewarding to every reader.

Fernand Van Steenberghen

It is our hope, therefore, that this small volume will be of value to historians of medieval philosophy, to medieval intellectual historians, and to all others who are interested in an up-to-date discussion of these topics by one of the world's foremost authorities on thirteenth-century philosophical thought.

In order not to make the following unduly cumbersome for a more general reading public, Professor Van Steenberghen has used relatively few footnotes. At the same time, he has provided all necessary references for those who may wish to examine in greater detail the matters discussed therein.

Original versions of Lectures I, II, and III were translated respectively by Professors Dominic J. O'Meara (The Catholic University of America), John F. Wippel (The Catholic University of America) and Stephen F. Brown (then of the University of the South, and now of Boston College). The additions to the three lectures were translated by Wippel, who is also responsible for editing and preparing the completed text for publication. Special thanks are due to Jude P. Dougherty, Dean of the University's School of Philosophy, for having arranged, with the full cooperation of the University's Administration, for Professor Van Steenberghen's visit to Washington, and for providing for the publication of this volume by The Catholic University of America Press.

John F. Wippel

THE FIRST LECTURE

ETERNITY OF THE WORLD

In these three lectures I have been asked to take as my topic the attitude adopted by Thomas Aquinas with respect to radical or heterodox Aristotelianism. I gladly accepted this suggestion, since in my opinion this stage in the history of doctrine, although happening seven centuries ago, is still of great interest to us and can teach us much concerning the solution to some of our contemporary problems.

Let me first remind you quickly of the historical circumstances which provoked the conflict between Thomas Aquinas and the proponents of radical Aristotelianism. Christianity was shaken in the thirteenth century by an event of great cultural importance—the massive importation of non-Christian philosophical literature which followed upon the enormous effort, intensified during the twelfth century, to translate Arabic and Greek texts into Latin. For the first time the Christian world discovered the impressive work of Aristotle, who then represented the summit of scientific knowledge, and many were conquered by the vision of the world proposed by the Philosopher. Despite the resistance of certain ecclesiastical authorities and of many theologians, who were aware of the danger which it constituted for Christian thought, Aristotelianism rapidly conquered the newly-founded universities of Western Europe. In Paris, a new statute of the Faculty of Arts, dated

1

March 19, 1255, placed all of the known writings of Aristotle on the lecture program, and this Faculty, which traditionally taught the seven liberal arts, became in practice a school of Aristotelian philosophy. Ten years later, the consequences of this innovation were felt. A group of young Masters, led by Siger of Brabant, taught the philosophy of Aristotle without concerning themselves with the points of opposition which exist between this philosophy and Christian doctrine. Radical or heterodox Aristotelianism was born.[1]

We still know very little about the beginnings of this school, since we have found few traces of its teaching before 1270. But we know that it existed and was already having a disturbing influence on the Faculty of Arts. This is what emerges, first from the protest of Saint Bonaventure in his Lenten sermons in 1267 and 1268, then from the intervention of Saint Thomas at the beginning of 1270 with the publication of his *De unitate intellectus*, and finally, from the first condemnation of this school by the Bishop of Paris, Stephen Tempier, on December 10, 1270.

What was Thomas Aquinas' role in the reaction against radical Aristotelianism? One may answer this question in two different ways: either by dealing with the concrete details of the controversy which broke out in 1270, or by taking a broader view of the doctrinal conflict between heterodox Aristotelianism and the work of Saint Thomas considered as a whole.

---

[1] On the introduction of Aristotelianism in the thirteenth century and on the rise of heterodox Aristotelianism see F. Van Steenberghen, *Aristotle in the West*, 2nd ed. (Louvain, 1970), pp. 59-208.

It is not possible for us to choose the first approach in a series of three public lectures, and for the following reasons. Thomas Aquinas returned to Paris in January, 1269. He first observed what the situation was in the schools and was informed about the teaching then being presented in the Faculty of Arts. It was only in the beginning of 1270 that he openly entered into conflict with Siger and his group. He remained in Paris until the spring of 1272, founded a Dominican studium in Naples in the fall of that same year, and taught there until December 6, 1273. If one wishes to study the concrete details of the controversy between Thomas Aquinas and Siger's group, one must examine, one by one, the works written by Thomas between 1270 and 1273, and one must try to find in these the traces of his reaction to radical Aristotelianism. Such long and laborious text analysis does not lend itself to oral exposition and would, in any case, require a large number of lectures. Moreover, we would have to discuss the fanciful views advanced by the young French Dominican, Father Édouard-Henri Wéber, in his work of 1970, *La controverse de 1270 à l'Université de Paris et son retentissement sur la pensée de saint Thomas d'Aquin.*

We must, therefore, choose the second approach, that of doctrinal history, although this choice will not prevent us from citing, when possible, from the writings of Siger and Thomas which pertain to the controversies of 1266-1273. Long before his return to Paris in 1269, Thomas Aquinas had identified what were, in his opinion, the most serious mistakes on the part of the pagan philosophies and the main points of opposition between these philosophies and Chris-

3

tian teaching. From the beginning of his career, in his *Scriptum super sententiis*, he opposed these positions. His thought did not evolve much subsequently on these points, with certain exceptions which we shall consider later, and these are the same mistaken positions which he found in the teaching of the heterodox Masters in 1269. I propose, then, to examine his attitude with respect to the three most important of these defended by radical Aristotelianism, namely, eternity of the world, monopsychism, and rationalism.

———————

In this first Lecture I shall concentrate on the problem of eternity of the world in the past. This lecture will have three parts. I shall first recall the position of non-Christian philosophy on this subject and illustrate it by the teaching of Siger of Brabant at the beginning of his career. I shall then describe Saint Thomas' reaction. Finally, I shall present some critical observations.

I

The first part can be dealt with rapidly, since it does no more than summarize some well-known facts. The problem as to the origin of the universe was already recognized at the beginnings of philosophy in Greece. Aristotle reports in Bk I of the *Physics* that the early philosophers (those now known as "Presocratics") assumed as evident that "nothing can come from what is not." From this they concluded that, since the world exists, it has always existed. To imagine that it began to be at a certain moment would be to imply that one day and on its own it emerged from what is not, which is absurd. In order to avoid affirming the eternity of the world in the past, these philosophers would have to have discovered the notion of a creative cause capable of giving existence to a world which could not exist without it. But these first Greek thinkers did not go beyond the level of a fairly rudimentary materialism and had no metaphysics of causality.

The thesis of the eternity of the world was taken up, with varying nuances, by all of Greek philosophy. But one may distinguish two periods in the history of Greek thought. Before Neoplatonism, it was thought that the material world had always existed because it was uncaused. Existing of itself, it exists necessarily and eternally. The work of Plotinus marks a crucial turning-point in the history of Greek thought. There the notion of metaphysical causality is introduced for the first time, in the form of the well-known doctrine of emanation. The One is really the *cause of the being* of all that emanates from it. But emanation is regarded as an eternal process, and hence the thesis of the eternity of the world is retained. This time the world is thought to be eternal because it is the necessary emanation from an eternal and unchanging cause.

The two greatest thinkers of Islam, Avicenna and Averroes, defended in somewhat different ways this view of the eternal world as the effect of an eternal cause. Only the Jewish thinkers, Avicebron and Moses Maimonides, rejected the eternalist position.

The Masters of the Faculty of Arts at Paris noted, therefore, this unanimous agreement on the part of

Greek and Arab philosophers concerning the origin of the universe. Hence it is not surprising that these Masters, impressed as they were by the consensus of earlier thinkers, were tempted to adopt this position themselves. This is, in fact, what one observes. At the beginning of his teaching career, before 1270, Siger of Brabant accepts without hesitation the eternity of the world.

In his *Quaestio utrum haec sit vera: "homo est animal", nullo homine existente*, Siger examines a difficulty which was classical in the Faculty of Arts (as is clear from various contemporary documents). This difficulty has to do with determining whether universal propositions treating of an abstract subject such as "man" are true independently of the existence of any concrete subject in which that abstract nature is realized. For example, under the hypothesis that no man exists (for instance, before man's appearance on earth), would the proposition "man is an animal" be true? Siger begins by presenting and rejecting five attempted solutions, the fourth of which he attributes to Albert of Cologne (Albert the Great). Then he offers his own solution. The hypothesis under consideration is itself absurd, since the human species, like every other species, is by its nature eternal. Therefore it is impossible for there ever to have been a moment when man did not exist.[2] As one can readily see, here Siger defends the eternity of the world without making any reference to the opposed teaching of the Church. This is why B. Bazán dates this *Quaestio* be-

---

[2] See B. Bazán, *Siger de Brabant. Écrits de logique, de morale et de physique*, Philosophes médiévaux XIV (Louvain-Paris, 1974), pp. 53-59.

fore the Condemnation of 1270, since after that date Siger always takes into account the demands of Christian belief.

Siger's *Quaestiones in tertium de anima* very probably date from 1269. They are certainly prior to the Condemnation of 1270.[3] These *Quaestiones* were not published in their entirety until 1972. Here Siger proposes a view of the human soul which is clearly inspired by Averroes and which is seriously at odds with Christian faith. But the heterodox character of his position does not seem to trouble him. So true is this, in fact, that one may wonder whether or not he is fully aware of it. As regards the origin of the intellect, which is unique for all mankind, Siger declares that according to Aristotle the human intellect is eternal because it is an immediate effect of the First Cause, which is itself eternal. Here he attributes to Aristotle the doctrine of creation, as Thomas Aquinas also does. According to Aristotle, as interpreted by Siger, to admit that the intellect was created in time would be to imply some change on the part of the divine will. This is why the Philosopher defended eternity of the world. However, adds Siger, Aristotle's position is not compelling, since the divine will remains mysterious for us, and who can understand it? God could have willed from eternity that the intellect would begin to be in the course of time, as Augustine maintained, for whom the human soul is created at the moment it is united to a body. But in the final analysis, Aristotle's position is more pro-

---

[3] See F. Van Steenberghen, *Maître Siger de Brabant*, Philosophes médiévaux XXI (Louvain-Paris, 1977), pp. 51-52.

bable than Augustine's since it corresponds better with the nature of the intellect, a separate substance. But be that as it may, one must choose here between Aristotle and Augustine, either one or the other.[4]

As the reader will note, in this discussion of the origin of the intellect Siger does not oppose the conclusions of philosophy to Christian teaching, but rather Aristotle's position to that of Augustine. These lectures on Bk III of the *De anima* do not betray any uneasiness of a religious nature. The young Master is taken with Aristotle and operates as a pure rationalist. He is unaware, or pretends to be unaware, of the dictates of Christian dogma. One may conclude, then, that it cannot be doubted that at the beginning of his teaching career Siger of Brabant accepted as his own the doctrine of eternity of the world.

One must recognize indeed that, at first sight, this vision of the world seems to be very plausible and even inevitable. If the existence of the world depends on an eternal creative act, how and why would the product of this act not be eternal? Besides, how could God create the world "in time," when time could not exist "before" the world or without the world? If God, eternal and unchanging, decides to create the world, what could prevent this world from being coeternal with its cause?

Now the Bible stands in opposition to this view of an eternal world. Already in the first verse of *Genesis* one reads: "In the beginning God created heaven and

---

[4] See B. Bazán, *Siger de Brabant. Quaestiones in tertium de anima. De anima intellectiva. De aeternitate mundi*, Philosophes médiévaux XIII (Louvain-Paris, 1972), pp. 4-8.

earth." This doctrine reappears in other scriptural texts and in commentators on scripture and teachers of the Law. And, later, Christian exegetes place this "beginning" back some thousands of years in the past.

Conflict was inevitable between this biblical teaching and pagan thought. The two conceptions had already clashed in the Patristic period and in the world of Islam, but the controversy took on new life in the thirteenth century in the Christian West.

II

Let us see now what Thomas Aquinas thought concerning this debate. He knew the pagan teaching of eternity of the world from the time of his studies in Cologne, at the school of Albert the Great, perhaps even from the time of his studies at the Faculty of Arts at the University of Naples prior to his entrance into the Dominican Order. And he adopted from the beginning of his teaching career an attitude which he maintained until his death. This attitude is characterized by two theses: (1) Revelation teaches us that the created world began to be; the world therefore is not eternal and the pagan position is false; (2) One cannot demonstrate by reason either the eternity of the world or that it began to be.

Let us note first that this was not a traditional position. Catholic theologians taught that the beginning of the world was not only a truth of faith, but also a rational certitude, and hence, that the eternalist position could be refuted philosophically. Recently Brother Bonaventure, Regent-Master of the Franciscans, had defended this in the Faculty of Theology at Paris.

Thomas Aquinas treated the problem of eternity of the world on many occasions. Here we shall pause to consider three points in his career: at the beginning in his *Scriptum super Sententiis* (1253-1257); then in the *Prima Pars* of the *Summa theologiae* (1266-1268); and finally in his opusculum *De aeternitate mundi* (probably ca. 1270).

Thomas began to comment on the *Sentences* in 1253, only three years after his Franciscan colleague, Bonaventure. The latter had maintained that the very idea of an eternal world created *ex nihilo* is self-contradictory and that no philosopher could have taught such an absurdity.[5] In Bk II of his own Commentary Thomas asserts, on the contrary, that the thesis of eternal creation (*ex nihilo*, since for him creation is defined as *productio ex nihilo*) is not contradictory and that we are unable to demonstrate by reason that the world began to be. Only faith in divine revelation teaches us that, in fact, the world had a temporal beginning.[6]

Here we shall not analyze in detail the long article which treats of this question. Thomas offers fourteen arguments in favor of eternity of the world and nine against it. In the corpus of the article he presents his agnostic position. One can demonstrate by reason neither the eternity nor the temporal beginning of the world. He then rejects in succession the argu-

---

[5] See *S. Bonaventura, Commentaria in quatuor libros Sententiarum*, II, dist. I, q. 2 (*Opera omnia*, t. II, p. 22).

[6] See *S. Thomas de Aquino, Scriptum super libros Sententiarum*, II, dist. 1, q. 1, art. 5 (ed. P. Mandonnet, [Paris, 1929], t. II, pp. 27-41).

ments for and the arguments against the world's eternity. His criticisms of arguments in support of eternity of the world are always to the point. As regards his criticisms of arguments against its eternity, one must, in my opinion, distinguish. In many cases his criticism is valid. Thus there is no incompatibility between "being created" and "existing from eternity." But when Thomas considers arguments based on the fact that, under the hypothesis of an eternal world, an infinite series of events will have been realized and that an infinite series cannot be realized, his replies are strangely confused and, in my opinion, inadequate. But we shall return to this later.

In the *Prima Pars* of the *Summa theologiae* one finds this same agnostic position, and it accounts for Thomas' division of the subject into two articles. The first shows that the arguments in favor of eternity of the world are without value, and the second does the same for the arguments against its eternity. In the first article Thomas maintains that for Aristotle the arguments which he proposed to establish the world's eternity were not strictly demonstrative. Their purpose was rather to refute some indefensible views of certain Presocratic philosophers. In fact both the existence and the duration of the universe depend upon the divine will, which enjoys supreme freedom. In the second article Thomas advances two arguments in order to justify his agnostic position. In the first he draws upon the Aristotelian theory of demonstration. The principle of demonstration is the essence, starting from which one deduces the properties of that essence. But essences abstract from space and time. Therefore, one cannot demonstrate that they have not always existed. In the second he appeals once more to divine freedom, which surpasses human understanding, in order to justify his agnostic attitude. In his reply to the objections he again encounters arguments based on the impossibility of infinite series, but dismisses them even more summarily than he had in his *Scriptum super Sententiis*.[7]

Let us now turn to Thomas' *De aeternitate mundi*. Father Mandonnet connects this treatise with the "Parisian Averroistic controversies," and Father Perrier has compounded his illustrious confrere's mistake by restating it in more precise terms.[8] In truth, it is enough for one to read this treatise to realize that it is not directed against the Averroists but rather against the conservative theologians who claimed that they could demonstrate by reason that the world had a beginning.[9] Certain manuscripts give to this opusculum a title which corresponds better to its content: *On the Possibility of the Eternity of the World (De possibilitate aeternitatis mundi)*.[10] Thomas here defends the view that a world eternally created by God does not entail any evident contradiction.

The problem is clearly formulated from the opening lines: "Granted then, in accord with Catholic belief, that the world has not always existed, but that

---

[7] See *Summa theologiae*, Iᵃ, q. 46, art. 1 and 2.

[8] See J. Perrier, *S. Thomae Aquinatis opuscula omnia...*, T. I. *Opuscula philosophica* (Paris, 1949), p. 52: "Valde probabile est illud pertinere ad disputationes contra Averroistas Parisienses."

[9] For the text see the Perrier edition, pp. 53-61; and more recently the critical edition published by the Leonine Commission in *Opera omnia*, v. 43 (1976), pp. 85-89.

[10] See M. Grabmann, *Die Werke des hl. Thomas von Aquin*, 3rd ed., *Beiträge zur Geschichte der Philosophie und Theologie des Mittelalters* 22, 1/2 (Münster, 1949), p. 341.

there was a beginning to its duration, the question has been raised as to whether it *could have* always existed." After a fairly long exposition intended to render precise the meaning of this question, Thomas concludes: "Therefore, the entire question consists in asking whether to be created by God according to its entire substance and to have no temporal beginning are contradictory or not." The contradiction could arise, he continues, from one of the two following principles (or from the two taken together): "an efficient cause must be prior to its effect;" and "it is necessary for a creature's nonbeing to precede its being in time, because the creature is produced from nothing (*ex nihilo*)." But neither of these two principles necessarily holds. As to the first, creative causality does not imply any kind of movement and is not, therefore, subject to time. One may liken it to instantaneous changes such as the illumination of a medium by light, wherein the cause and the effect are simultaneous with one another. As to the second principle, the expression "made from nothing" (*factum ex nihilo*) really means "not made from something" (*factum non ex aliquo*). It simply signifies that a creature is not produced from a pre-existing subject, as when we say of someone that he is worried about "nothing" when he is worried without any reason. The expression "from nothing" (*ex nihilo*) does not, therefore, signify "after nothing" (*post nihilum*), unless one gives to the word "after" (*post*) the meaning of priority of nature rather than temporal priority. In fact, of its nature a created being is nothing. It receives being from its cause and would not be if its cause did not give being to it.

13

There is, therefore, no repugnance between being created and always existing. If there were any such repugnance between these two notions, it would be surprising that Augustine overlooked this when he was contending against the eternity of the world by numerous arguments. It would be equally surprising that the most eminent philosophers failed to see this repugnance. And Thomas concludes ironically: "Therefore those who see this contradiction with such subtlety are alone worthy to be called men and with them is wisdom born."

When authorities such as John Damascene or Hugh of Saint-Victor say that nothing can be coeternal with God, one must understand them in the light of Boethius. God alone is immutable and, therefore, the eternity of the world would be quite different from divine eternity. This interpretation is fully confirmed by different passages in St. Augustine.

Thomas ends by recalling the well-known objection based on an infinite number of human souls. If the world were eternal (and, with it, all species), an infinite multitude of men would have existed and their immortal souls would subsist as an infinite multitude. This is a more difficult objection, concedes Aquinas, but it is not decisive. For God could have created an eternal world without the human species, or he could have created the human race at a certain moment of that temporal duration which would characterize the course of the eternal world. Moreover, no one has yet demonstrated that God could not create a world in which an infinite multitude of human souls would exist.

His treatise ends with this statement: "At this time

I forbear to reply to other objections, either because I have already done so elsewhere, or because some of them are so weak that by their very weakness they seem to reinforce the probability of the opposite position."

Why did Thomas Aquinas adopt this "agnostic" attitude? He indicates this clearly on many occasions. He was struck by the weakness of the arguments offered in favor of the beginning of the world and fears that reasonings so poor, presented to establish an article of faith, would invite mockery from nonbelievers. Already in Bk II of the *Sentences* he writes: "all these arguments have been refuted by the philosophers; hence to wish to ground oneself on such reasons to prove, against the philosophers, that the world began to be, would result more in contempt for the faith than in confirmation of it." The same idea reappears twelve years later in the *Summa theologiae*: "That the world began is an object of faith and not of science. It is useful to see this, for fear that someone, attempting to demonstrate what is an object of faith, might propose non-cogent arguments, giving to nonbelievers cause for mockery, since they would think that we believed for such futile reasons."

However, behind this so clearly expressed reason appears another less explicitly formulated. Thomas Aquinas was himself also impressed by the unanimous agreement of the great Greek and Arabic thinkers. One can gather this already from the text of the *Sentences* that I have just quoted. "Against the philosophers," he says. It is the unanimous conviction of the philosophers that one contradicts in affirming that the world had a beginning. And we have seen that in his *De aeternitate mundi*, Thomas could not hide his impatience with the pretentious attitude of those theologians who saw an evident contradiction between the fact of being created and the fact of existing eternally.

Were the arguments of the theologians really as weak as Saint Thomas maintains? These arguments can be grouped into two principal types. We find both types in Saint Bonaventure, who was a colleague of St. Thomas in the Faculty of Theology at Paris from 1252 until 1257. The first kind of argument is based on the notion of creation. To be created "from nothing" (*ex nihilo*) and to exist eternally would be two contradictory propositions. This type of argument rests on a confusion between "from nothing" (*ex nihilo*) and "after nothing" (*post nihilum*). Thomas is right in rejecting it as ineffectual. But another type of argument is based on the fact that an eternal world would imply an infinite series of completed events. But the notion of an infinite realized series is untenable, since it involves many contradictions.

At first glance, it seems Thomas would welcome this type of argument, for, in a well-known article in the beginning of the *Summa theologiae* (*Prima Pars*, q. 7, art. 4), he rejects as impossible every infinite multitude *in act*. Only an infinite *in potency* is possible, and by "infinite in potency" he here means a finite series which increases indefinitely. He cites as examples the indefinite division of a continuum and the indefinite addition of units to a number. According to this terminology, the infinite series of past events implied by the hypothesis of an eternal world is clearly an infinite in act, not an infinite in potency. Indeed, it is a realized and achieved infinite, already produced in reality. It would have been enough for Saint Thomas to keep to this clear doctrine in order to condemn the eternalist thesis since, as all agreed, that implies a real succession of an infinite series of past events. According to the teaching of Question 7, such an infinite series would not be "numerable" at all, not even for God's thought. It would be foreign to every "species" of multitude. Such a series could not be an object of the Creator's will.

However, when Thomas takes up the problem of the origin of the world in Question 46 of the *Prima Pars*, he seems to forget the thesis he had so clearly presented in Question 7. Now he maintains, being directly inspired by Aristotle's *Physics*, that a world eternal as to its past would not imply an infinite in act, but only an infinite in potency. Why? Because past events were successive and therefore were never realized all together (*simul*). As we see, the notions of the infinite are now modified. The infinite in act becomes the actual or simultaneous infinite. The infinite in potency is no longer the finite which increases indefinitely, but the infinite in succession.

Understandably, opponents of the eternalist thesis viewed this shift in the meaning of the infinite in potency as nothing but an evasion. They refused to admit that the infinite in succession may be considered as an infinite in potency. By means of an irrefutable *ad hominem* argument, they showed that an infinite in succession, without being an "actual" or "simultaneous" infinite, is truly an infinite in act. Indeed, for Aristotle all species are eternal. There was never a "first man," and an infinity of individuals have succeeded one another in the past. But human souls are immortal. Consequently, in the case of the human species an infinite in succession becomes a simultaneous infinite. An infinity in act of human souls would exist today, and what is even more absurd, this infinite series would increase every day with the birth of new individuals!

Saint Thomas encounters this objection several times during his career and recognizes its difficulty. Yet he always tries to escape from it, as we have seen above in his *De aeternitate mundi*. There he seems to forget completely his demonstration in Question 7 of the *Prima Pars* of the *Summa*.

III

In the third part of this Lecture I should like to present to you some of my personal reflections and some critical comments. What should one make of this debate concerning the origins of the universe? How should one evaluate Thomas Aquinas' contribution to this controversy? We may first note that Thomas knows well the position of the major Greek and Arabic philosophers, and especially that of Aristotle. He rejects this position in the name of Christian faith. Secondly, we must remember that he always maintained that one cannot demonstrate by reason that the world began to be.

But on closer inspection, one notices strange variations in his statements concerning the infinite. Sometimes he rejects every infinite in act, whether simultaneous or in succession. Sometimes he rejects only the infinite in simultaneous act. And sometimes he admits the possibility of an infinite simultaneously in act. Rarely, indeed, does one find such variations in the work of the Angelic Doctor, whose thought is usually so firm and consistent.

As for us, we must choose between these three irreconcilable positions. For my part, I do not hesitate to follow the Thomas of the *Summa theologiae*, *Prima Pars*, q. 7, where he expresses himself freely without being troubled by the problem of the eternity of the world.

It may be useful for me to tell you something about the historical background for my choice. In my youth I had as Professor of Cosmology the venerable Canon Désiré Nys, one of the first collaborators of Cardinal Mercier, founder of the Thomistic school of Louvain. Nys was convinced of the possibility of an eternal world and of infinite series in space and in time. But his enthusiastic explanations always seemed to me playing with words. He was so good at juggling with infinite series that he caused considerable mirth among his students. The following year, another professor, Canon Léon Becker, Professor of Theodicy, rejected with equal conviction every kind of quantitative infinity, and rested his case on Question 7 of the *Prima Pars*, where Thomas explains clearly why every real multitude must be finite. Since that time I have been convinced that this is correct and therefore that eternity of the world in the past is absolutely impossible. This I shall now attempt to explain to you.

Let us first recall Thomas' argumentation in Question 7 of the *Prima Pars*. He offers two arguments to show why every infinite multitude in act is impossible.

First of all, any existing multitude must be included in a determinate species, for, as Aristotle has shown, it is not possible to be in a genus without also being in a species. But the species of multitude correspond to the species of number. And no species of number is infinite since every number is a plurality measured by unity. An infinite multitude in act is therefore impossible, for it would be an indeterminate and indistinct multitude, foreign to every species of multitude. The second argument is equally rigorous. Every existing multitude in the real world is created. But every created reality is the terminus of a determinate intention of the Creator, since no agent acts without an end (a fortiori the infinitely wise agent which is the Creator). It is therefore necessary that all created things constitute a determined or definite number, and hence impossible for there to be an infinite multitude in act.

On the other hand, there is nothing to prevent the existence of an infinite multitude in potency, that is to say, of a finite multitude capable of increasing indefinitely without ever becoming infinite in act. In the preceding article, where Thomas also rejects all infinite spatial magnitude, he notes that the infinite dealt with in mathematics is always the infinite in potency, that is to say, the indefinite or the finite which increases indefinitely.

This doctrine seems enlightening to me and its application to the problem of the universe's past equally clear. However, a possible source of misunderstanding must first be eliminated. So long as one thinks merely of the being of the universe, that is, the universe as a substance or a set of substances, it makes

20

no sense to say that it "began" to exist "at a moment in time" or "in time." This would be to imagine a time existing before the world as an autonomous entity. The only question which arises concerning the order of finite substances is whether or not this order is caused. But the universe is not inert since the finite substances which constitute it are essentially active. Therefore, the universe is subject to perpetual evolution, the source of many and varied movements or changes, and the question arises: Did this evolution have a beginning point?

This is the real problem raised by the universe's past. Here again it is not a question as to whether evolution began "in time" or "at a certain moment in time," as if time existed before the world. This was Kant's mistake when he formulated his "first antinomy." He thought that one who affirms the "beginning" of the world presupposes a prior existence of time. In short he repeated the faulty argument by which Aristotle claimed to demonstrate the eternity of time, an argument which was repeatedly refuted in the Middle Ages. The true question is simply to determine whether or not the evolution of the universe had a beginning, whether or not there was for each created substance a first activity, a first becoming.

Once one has understood that a quantitative infinite in act is an impossibility, there can be no doubt concerning the answer to the question just raised. Evolution had a beginning, for an evolution without a beginning, without a first, without a point of departure, would be infinite, which is absolutely impossible. With the evolution of the universe time began, since time is defined as the measure of motion or of change.

It is interesting to note that recent developments in the natural sciences confirm the idea of a point of departure for evolution. The world of antiquity was a world without history, eternally subject to the same physical laws determined by the circular, uniform, and perpetual movement of the heavenly spheres around our planet. Modern science presents a very different picture of the cosmos. This is evident in biology. Life appeared on earth at a certain determinate period in the past. And several well-known physical systems now extend the idea of evolution to the material universe as a whole and assign a point of departure to this evolution. This evidently raises new problems, which the methods of the positive sciences cannot resolve. Here they must yield the field to the philosophers. But it is highly suggestive to observe that contemporary science is turning towards a view which rejoins that of the philosophers who were opposed to the eternity of the world.

How is one to account for the strange variations which we found in St. Thomas concerning the infinite? As for myself, I find no other explanation than his extraordinary respect for Aristotle, whose authority regarding the eternity of the world was confirmed by the unanimous agreement of the great Greek and Arabic philosophers. As I have indicated, it is in Aristotle's *Physics* that Thomas found the idea that the infinite in succession is an infinite in potency. The Stagirite, who was forced into affirming eternity of the world because he did not know the doctrine of creation, but who also rejected without reservation the infinite in act, found this means of escape in his attempt to reconcile the two theses: eternity of the world, and the impossibility of an infinite in act. St. Thomas took up this notion that an infinite in succession is not an infinite in act.

That Thomas abandoned the solid teaching of Question 7 under Aristotle's influence is confirmed by the curious weakness of the positions he defends in Question 46 when he discusses the origin of the world.

This emerges first from a study of the two arguments which he offers in the corpus of article 2 in order to justify his agnostic thesis that one cannot rationally demonstrate that the world began to be. In the first argument he calls upon the Aristotelian theory of demonstration, as we have seen above (pp. 11-12). It is surprising that Thomas did not recognize the weakness of this argument. He well knows that besides the kind of demonstration which Aristotle proposes as perfect demonstration, there are other types of valid demonstration: for instance, demonstrating a cause from an effect, the only kind of demonstration which makes it possible to prove God's existence. He should have shown that no type of demonstration can enable one to prove that the world began. Moreover, even a demonstration starting from essence would be possible, since he himself in Question 7 had proved the impossibility of an infinite in act from the essence of multitude. And from this impossibility it would have been easy to deduce the impossibility of an eternal past. In the second argument he appeals to the divine freedom, whose mystery transcends human reason. We cannot know whether

God willed to create an eternal or a temporal world. But in Question 7 he had shown that the divine will cannot have as its object any infinite multitude, a fact which evidently rules out an infinite series of past events.

The same weakness appears in Thomas' replies to some of the objections which he raised against himself at the beginning of the article. In the interests of brevity, I shall consider only the sixth, which is the most typical and which might be a reply to Bonaventure's strongest argument against the eternity of the world. This warrants closer study. Bonaventure took as a concrete example the celestial revolutions, a fundamental element of Aristotelian cosmology which was universally accepted in the thirteenth century. According to Aristotle the heavenly spheres revolve eternally around the earth, and these revolutions determine the divisions of time into years, months, and days. The Franciscan Master put the following dilemma to defenders of eternity of the world. Are all the past revolutions at a finite (and hence numerable) distance from the present revolution, or are certain revolutions infinitely distant from the present one? If one chooses the first alternative, one concedes that the world began, since the furthermost revolution is still at a finite distance from the present one. It is therefore the first and with it cosmic evolution began. If one chooses the second alternative, affirming that at least one past revolution is at an infinite distance from the present one, what is the situation with respect to the revolution which immediately follows it? If this is at a finite distance, the same must be said concerning the preceding one, since it differs from it by only one unit (a unit added to the finite cannot produce the infinite!). One must then say that the succeeding revolution is also at an infinite distance. But then the same problem arises with respect to the third revolution, and then with the fourth and so on. In short, on this hypothesis it is not possible to account for the transition from infinitely distant revolutions to those which we know and which are clearly at a finite distance from the present day.

The value of demonstrations such as these is that they are proofs by means of the absurd. The hypothesis of the eternity of the world is shown to imply absurd consequences and is thus itself absurd. This is an important method, since many do not immediately understand that a quantitative infinite is impossible. They adopt the hypothesis of an eternal world and consequently of an infinite series of events without any beginning point. Then they take refuge in the mystery of the infinite in order to ward off all objections raised against them, just like a warship which, when threatened by the enemy, surrounds itself with a thick artificial fog. Fortunately, however, there is one way of refuting them—to show that their hypotheses involve absurd consequences. This is what Bonaventure does in the argument described above.

According to Professor A. Zimmermann, distinguished Director of the Thomas-Institut in Cologne, Thomas responded to Bonaventure's objection in his reply to objection 6 in Question 46, art. 2. This is debatable, but, if this is the case, Thomas' reply appears to me to be inadequate. According to objection 6, if the world has always existed, an infinity of days has preceded the present one (that is to say, today). But it is not possible to traverse the infinite. Therefore, it would have been impossible to reach the present day. What is Thomas' reply? There is no "traversing," he says, but that from one point to another. Whatever day in the past is designated, from that point to the present the distance is always finite and can, therefore, be traversed.

A surprising and totally unsatisfactory reply! Whatever day in the past is "designated," he says, is at a finite distance from today. That is evident, because, since I could not designate (*signare*) an infinitely distant day, such a day would be completely unknowable to me. But then I in turn propose a dilemma. Can one designate each of the days which have really existed in the past without exception? If the reply is *yes*, one concedes that the world began since all past days without exception are at a finite distance from the present one, and therefore the furthermost day is the first day. If the reply is *no*, one then concedes that one or more days are at an infinite distance from today and falls into Bonaventure's trap.

Let us end this first lecture with a brief conclusion. Thomas Aquinas, like all his contemporaries, had to face the unanimous affirmation of the Greek and Arabic philosophers along with certain Masters in the Arts Faculty at Paris to this effect, that the world is eternal in the past. Like all Catholic theologians he always rejected eternity of the world because of his faith. But, contrary to most of the theologians, he unceasingly maintained that the beginning of the world could not be rationally demonstrated. Yet he had formulated some excellent principles concerning the impossibility of any infinite in act. But the authority of the great philosophers prevented him from applying these principles to the case of the origin of the world.

The controversy which I have here described is not just an academic discussion. It has important metaphysical and even religious repercussions. For when one clearly understands that the material universe could not be eternal, but that its evolution and, consequently, its very being, had a beginning, one realizes immediately that this universe could not be without a cause, as is still alleged today by materialistic philosophers. It depends for its very being on a cause which transcends matter and evolution. Here one has an interesting path towards the discovery of God as creator of the universe.

THE SECOND LECTURE

MONOPSYCHISM

The second important questionable position defended by radical Aristotelianism, and one that Thomas Aquinas unceasingly opposed, is monopsychism. You are undoubtedly familiar with this term. It refers to that doctrine according to which there is only one immaterial soul for all of mankind, and, as a consequence, only one intellect. This collective soul is therefore the true subject of thought. When an individual believes that he himself is thinking, in fact it is rather the unique soul for the human species that thinks in him by using his brain images (*phantasmata*) in order to abstract ideas therefrom.

This doctrine was first formulated by the Arab philosopher, Averroes, who lived at Córdoba in Spain in the twelfth century. It was revived in the thirteenth century by certain Masters of the Arts Faculty at Paris and then, at the beginning of the fourteenth century, by John of Jandun and his Parisian school. Finally, the same doctrine was taught for many centuries by the Italian Averroists of Bologna and Padua. Monopsychism is, therefore, a typical Averroistic doctrine and, to the extent that they defended this same position, the radical Aristotelians deserve to be called "Averroists."

At first sight it is difficult to understand how a doctrine so strange, so contrary to psychological experience as well as to fundamental dogmas of Christianity, could have been taught with conviction by certain Christian Masters for many centuries. As we shall see, this is to be explained both by reason of the extraordinary regard these Masters had for Aristotle, and by their equally great regard for metaphysical values even when they seem to run counter to the data of experience.

This lecture will once more include three parts. I shall first describe the origins and the nature of monopsychism. This exposition will be illustrated by a concrete example, the *Quaestiones in tertium de anima* of Siger of Brabant. Then I shall present Thomas Aquinas' reaction to this curious position, especially by concentrating on an analysis of his *De unitate intellectus*. Finally, I shall conclude with some critical reflections about this controversy.

I

Monopsychism finds its historical origins in Aristotle's philosophy. The Stagirite was unaware of the doctrine of creation. As a consequence he viewed the universe as an eternal hierarchical order that is necessary in itself and includes two subordinated worlds radically different in nature, the higher or celestial world and the lower or earthly world. The higher world consists of eternal substances, each of which forms a distinct species. In this celestial world there are, on the one hand, the transparent heavenly spheres which revolve around the earth and each of which bears one or more heavenly body, that is to say, the planets and the fixed stars; and there are, on the other hand, the immaterial movers of the spheres, among which the highest is the First Mover or the absolutely Unmoved Mover, which moves the entire universe by attraction or insofar as it is an object of love, that is to say, as a final cause of all the movements of the universe. The lower or sublunary world, on the contrary, consists of substances that are subject to generation and corruption. While species themselves are eternal, individuals succeed one another in time. In order to guarantee the permanence of the species, individuals therein can reproduce and multiply because of prime matter, the principle of individuation and of purely numerical multiplication of the specific perfection. In this lower world only prime matter is eternal and uncaused.

In such a universe the problem of human nature was bound to raise insurmountable difficulties for Aristotle. The Stagirite regarded thinking as one of man's activities and the intellect (*nous*) as a part of the soul, that is to say, a part of the principle of life in man. Moreover, the intellect is man's specific difference, since he is defined as a "rational animal." And in the *Nicomachean Ethics*, intellectual contemplation is described as man's ultimate perfection. But at the same time the Philosopher stresses the immaterial nature of thought and of the intellect which is its principle. Being immaterial, the intellect cannot be generated by the substantial change of matter. And in fact, in a celebrated passage in his treatise *On the Generation of Animals* Aristotle states that the intellect in man "comes from without" (literally: "through the door"). How is one to reconcile all of this? Man clearly belongs to the category of corruptible corporeal substances and to the genus "animal." He is therefore composed of matter and form, of body and soul. He is born and he dies like all animals. But the intellect as immaterial and inorganic seems to belong to another world, that of immaterial substances which are eternal, simple, and each of which is unique in its species. How is such an intellect to be united with the individual human being? From whence does such an intellect come? How can it constitute man's specific perfection? What becomes of it at the death of the individual man? Does each human individual possess his own intellect? If so, how can this immaterial substance be multiplied within one and the same species? These questions cannot be resolved within the framework of Aristotle's metaphysics. To what extent did he recognize them? We cannot say, but one thing is certain. He had the wisdom to leave these questions unresolved rather than to involve himself in hypotheses that run counter to experience. And this attests both to his common sense and to his genius.[1]

But his prudence was to lead to unending controversies on the part of his disciples down through the centuries, first among the Greeks, then among Arab and Jewish thinkers, and finally within the Christian world. Time will not permit us to recall here the long history of these controversies and the many solutions proposed for the enigmas of Aristotle's *Treatise on the Soul* (*De anima*). I shall limit myself to one observation, both because it is important and because I have not found it in the historians who have studied these controversies. To the extent that Aristotle's disciples are influenced by Neoplatonism, to that extent do they escape from the difficulties of his psychology, and this because they abandon the rigid framework of his

---

[1] Cf. F. Van Steenberghen, *Aristotle in the West*, pp. 10-15.

metaphysics. This fact is quite striking in Avicenna. Because of his theory of emanation he sees no difficulty in saying that many immaterial souls emanate from the Tenth Intelligence and unite themselves to the various human bodies generated here below. But somewhat later Averroes reacts strongly against these "deviations" on Avicenna's part and returns to a much more authentic Aristotelianism. Immediately, all of the antinomies of the *De anima* reappear.

In truth there are only two possible ways of escaping from the impasse in which Aristotle's psychology finds itself. One may remain within the framework of Aristotle's metaphysics and then one ends in monopsychism. This is the path followed by Averroes. Or else one may start from the psychological analyses of the *De anima* and the *Ethics* and correct the metaphysical deficiencies of the Stagirite by appealing to the doctrine of creative causality. This is the way chosen by Thomas Aquinas.

Let us first consider Averroes' solution. His fundamental thesis is simple and perfectly logical. Aristotle, he maintains, has demonstrated that intellection is an inorganic activity and immaterial in nature. The principle of intellection or the intellective soul is therefore an immaterial substance. But, according to Aristotle, an immaterial substance is eternal, ungenerated and incorruptible, and unique in its species. Therefore the intellective soul is an eternal substance and unique for all mankind.

Once this fundamental thesis has been established (which a Paris Master of Siger's school will accurately style the *fundamentum Commentatoris*), Averroes must explain how intellectual activity on the part of this separate and unique substance can become in some way the activity of individual human beings. For one must account for the fact that we have at least the impression of engaging in thinking. Averroes must explain how he himself could write his learned books and discuss therein the view of other philosophers whose positions differed from his own. The single intellect evidently thinks in different ways in different individuals. Averroes diligently attempts to account for all of these facts. His central point is this. The single intellect is naturally ordered toward individual human beings. It unites itself to them in their brains by making use of their cerebral images in order to abstract ideas therefrom and it uses these ideas in order to think in them. It is in this way that the activity of the single intellect takes place in different fashion in different individuals, and each individual has the impression that he is thinking when in fact the intellect for the whole species thinks in him by using his images.

Certain Masters of the Faculty of Arts at Paris had been won over to the Averroistic interpretation of the *De anima* during the decade that runs from 1260 to 1270. It seemed to them that this was the only way of doing justice to the great principles of Aristotelian metaphysics, in particular to this fundamental law: An immaterial substance is unique within its species, separate from matter and eternal. Such is the situation with respect to the intellective human soul.

What is striking in this attitude is the extraordinary attachment on the part of its defenders to what they regarded as intangible metaphysical values. One is here at the opposite pole from the empiricist mentality, so widespread today, and especially in America. As I have already indicated, it is this respect for metaphysical values, joined with an unswerving fidelity to the authority of Aristotle, that accounts for the survival of the Averroistic school until the beginning of the seventeenth century.

But let us return to the first "Averroists" of the Faculty of Arts at Paris. We still know very little about the beginnings of this school before 1270. As regards monopsychism, until now we have only one direct source for this fundamentally heterodox doctrine — Siger of Brabant's *Quaestiones in tertium de anima* (*Questions on Bk III of the De anima*). This work, which we have already cited with respect to the eternity of the world,[2] was published in its entirety in 1972. What we have is not Siger's own redaction but a *reportatio* of the Master's lectures, that is to say, notes taken by an auditor during his lectures. There are solid reasons for dating these lectures in 1269.

The position which Siger presents here coincides substantially with that of Averroes. There is only one agent intellect and only one possible (that is to say, receiving) intellect for all mankind. These intellects are not united to individual men by their substance, but only by their activity. When we have the impression that we ourselves are thinking, it is really the possible intellect which thinks in us with the aid of our brain images. Let us follow our philosopher in his development of this Averroist doctrine.

Siger's *Quaestiones* form a small, well-constructed treatise, divided into four parts, which treat respec-

---

[2] See above, pp. 7-8.

tively of the differences between the intellect and the other parts of the soul, the nature of the intellect in itself, the relationship of the intellect to human bodies, and the intellect's powers of operation.

In the first part the author considers only one question. Is the intellective principle "rooted" in the same substance as the vegetative and sensitive principles?[3] At first sight this wording is reassuring since in the preceding lines the intellect has twice been referred to as "part" of the soul in that it was compared to "other parts of the soul." One therefore has the impression that for Siger the intellect truly belongs to the soul of the individual. But we shall soon see that this favorable impression is not well grounded.

The problem under consideration had divided the Scholastics for quite some time, since two divergent positions had developed during the first half of the century. These may be roughly described as the view of the philosophers and the view of the theologians. The philosophers ordinarily admitted the existence of at least *two souls* in man — a vegetative-sensitive soul "drawn from the potency of matter" and the terminus of natural generation, and an immaterial intellective soul which is created immediately by God either at the moment of conception or during the course of the development of the embryo. The theologians, on the other hand, usually defended the existence of *only one soul*, which is the principle of all of man's activities because of its three powers of operation.

---

[3] "Utrum intellectivum radicatur in eadem animae substantia cum vegetativo et sensitivo" (Bazán ed., p. 1).

Albert the Great had first defended the view of the theologians in his *Summa de creaturis* (ca. 1240-1245). But he had proposed a new position in his *De natura et origine animae*, undoubtedly written after 1260. The intellective soul, created by God, is united to the vegetative-sensitive soul which itself is progressively formed in the embryo. The intellective soul constitutes with the latter one single composite substance, which is partly of internal origin and partly of external origin (*partim ab intrinseco et partim ab extrinseco*). The same position is presented in the anonymous *Quaestiones de anima* which have been published by J. Vennebusch and which he dates around 1260.[4]

This brief historical summary will serve to clarify Siger's position in the first question of his treatise. In presenting the human soul as a *composite* soul, he remains within the "philosophical" tradition and one might believe that he is defending an entirely traditional position. But let us examine this more closely.

After he has rejected the opinion of the theologians, Siger states that the intellect, having come from without, unites with the vegetative and sensitive principle. By this union the *human soul* itself is constituted, which is a composite soul. Here Siger seems to admit of a substantial bond between the two components of the human soul, which would in turn imply duality of substantial forms in man: the intellective soul, and the vegetative-sensitive soul. But this interpretation is excluded by later questions in the treatise where he

---

[4] On the history of this problem see J. M. da Cruz Pontes, "Le problème de l'origine de l'âme de la patristique à la solution thomiste," *Recherches de théologie ancienne et médiévale* 31 (1964), pp. 197-227.

professes the most classical kind of Averroism. The intellect is a single separate substance. It cannot be the substantial form of the body (q. 7), but perfects (*perficit*) it by its power of operation which is united to the individual's power of operation, his imagination. Moreover, it is because the intellect is a separate substance that it is unique and eternal (qq. 9 and 2). There can be no question, therefore, of a true substantial union in the treatise's first question.

The second part studies the nature of the intellect in itself. The intellect is *eternal*, at least if one holds to Aristotle's opinion (which we have discussed in the previous lecture).[5] Hence it is *ungenerated*. Among commentators on Aristotle, only Alexander of Aphrodisias had defended the opposed position. But we are conscious of receiving universal forms (ideas) in ourselves. Since a material power can only grasp material objects, that is to say, individuals, the intellect is therefore an immaterial reality and cannot be generated.

Ungenerated, the intellect is also *incorruptible* by its nature. However, since it is finite, it does not have of itself the power to exist perpetually. It owes its perpetual character to its Cause, which in creating it also gives to it the capacity to endure forever. But this capacity is dependent upon the divine will.

Finally, the intellect is *not composed of matter and form*. At the conclusion of a long and interesting discussion with defenders of spiritual matter, Siger excludes all matter from the intellect. It is composed only of genus and a specific difference.

---

[5] See above, pp. 7-8.

The third part, which considers the single intellect's relation to the plurality of human bodies, is most important, since Siger here unveils clearly his Averroist positions. The intellect perfects the body not by its substance but by its power of operation. Its union with the body is therefore by operation, not substantial. In what does this union by operation consist? It is twofold. As a mover of the body the intellect moves the entire body *per se* and every part of the body *per accidens.* As principle of intellection, the intellect is united only to the imagination (*phantasia*) and to its organ, the brain. As a separate substance, the intellect is *unique* for the entire human species. Moreover, since the intellect is incorruptible, the species is adequately represented by one single intellect, as is true of all separate substances. But its activity varies in different individuals because each presents to the unique intellect its own cerebral images (*phantasmata*).

In the fourth part Siger considers the two powers of the intellect and their activity. It is here that the insurmountable difficulties of the Averroist position come to the surface, and Siger examines these with great loyalty. First of all, is the intellect passive in its activity? It is not passive in the way in which matter is, but it is *receptive.* It is of itself in potency to the intelligible representations which it receives. But if, like every immaterial reality, it is impassible, can it suffer from fire? Hardly a philosophical question, notes Siger, since it obviously refers to the fire of hell, a matter of concern to theology rather than philosophy. Nonetheless, our philosopher considers this issue because he sees in the theologians' explanations certain points which do not appear to be in harmony with philosophical theses. He could have immediately avoided the problem by appealing to his Averroist positions. The single intellective soul for all mankind is never in the condition of a separate soul, since it is always united to the many individuals in whom it exercises its intellectual activity. In a word, according to the Averroist point of view, the question of sanctions in the life to come does not even arise and the problem of hell-fire is simply a false problem. But before arriving at this conclusion, Siger permits himself the pleasure of criticizing different views held by the theologians.

As we said, the intellect is receptive, in potency. How then does it pass into act? By the action of the agent intellect, which produces ideas by abstraction from our images and "informs" the receptive intellect with them. The receptive intellect first grasps first principles in an infallible manner, and then all else in light of these first principles. The receptive intellect always knows the agent intellect, but is not united to us in this higher kind of knowledge. We know of the existence of the agent intellect because we have a certain experience of the fact that the receptive intellect receives abstract ideas. This reveals to us the abstractive activity of the agent intellect.

But all of this raises certain difficulties, which Siger himself lists. How can the agent intellect produce a multiplicity of intelligibles in an intellect which is simple, immaterial, and inorganic? How can the intellect's operation be regarded as our own, if the intellect itself is united to us only by means of our images, which are nothing but the matter for intellection?

40

These questions give rise to a lengthy discussion which is quite interesting. In substance Siger's reply is this. The intellect's operation becomes ours in some way because by its nature the intellect has need of our images in order to exercize its activities. This is why Averroes shows that the union of this unique and eternal intellect with the human species, which is also unique and eternal, is more essential than its union with any particular individual.

But Siger is too intelligent to be satisfied with this reply. In the following lecture he sums up the difficulties he has encountered before, and this time presents them as threefold. How is the unique intellect united with us? How can this intellect's knowing be diversified in different human individuals? If the intellect is a separate substance, why does it have need of corporeal images? Here are the essentials of his response. Our union with the intellect is a fact, since we are conscious of possessing in ourselves the contents of abstract thought. Since this union cannot be substantial, we must conclude that it is only by way of operation. There is another fact. Intellectual activity is realized in different ways in different individuals. This fact can only be explained by reason of the different images which are present in different brains. But it is difficult to explain how our images can serve as a bond between ourselves and the intellect, since they cease to be images once they become ideas in the intellect. Siger finds no other explanation but the fact that the intellect is naturally united to us. It is of its nature to draw its ideas from our images.

Since the intellect is a separate substance for Siger, he does not go beyond the limits of his treatise by raising two questions relating to the knowledge enjoyed by separate substances. First of all, do they know themselves? And secondly, do separate substances know one another? A separate substance knows itself because it is an intelligible in act. It is not singularity but matter which presents an obstacle to thought. But one separate substance cannot know another one because, according to Aristotle, a separate substance knows only by knowing its own substance. Such knowledge may reveal to it the existence of either its cause or its effect. But separate substances are not related to one another as cause and effect. Therefore, they cannot know one another. But they do know the First Cause, precisely because they are its effects.

Siger raises a final question. Can the intellect know the particular? This question was much debated during the thirteenth century. He explains that a certain knowledge of the particular is possible because the content of a universal idea is realized in the particular which that idea represents. But the intellect cannot know a particular *in forma propria*, that is to say, in that which formally constitutes its individuality.

Here we have, to be sure, a radically heterodox interpretation of Aristotelian psychology. Siger sets forth these positions so subversive to religion without any apparent scruple. However, at times he does experience some hesitation with respect to his Averroist theses, and he acknowledges this with the same frankness. His behavior betrays the marks of his youthfulness — levity, intransigence, audacity. But the young Master will soon encounter opposition from the theologians as well as censure by ecclesiastical authority.

He will emerge from that conflict as more mature and more prudent. In sum, then, the *Quaestiones in tertium de anima* reveal a young Master who is bold but also loyal, one who is deeply impressed by Aristotle, and one who sees in Averroes the best interpreter of the Stagirite's psychology.[6]

II

One may ask, what was Thomas Aquinas' reaction to monopsychism? In order to reply to this question I shall first present a brief overview of the anthropology which Thomas developed, in large part in order to meet the challenge of Averroes. Then I shall analyze his small treatise, *De unitate intellectus*, which he wrote in 1270 against Siger of Brabant and other Parisian defenders of Averroist monopsychism.[7]

As I indicated in my first lecture, St. Thomas was aware of the major shortcomings of Greek and Arabic philosophy from the beginning of his career. Thus one finds in Bk II of his Commentary on the *Sentences* (dating ca. 1255) a noteworthy historical exposition on the problem of the intellect (Dist. 17, q. 2, a. 1) in which Averroes' monopsychism is explained and criticized at length. This indicates that by that time Thomas had developed his own anthropology. I say "his own anthropology" because here, as in so many other areas, his thought is quite original and personal.

---

[6] For a more complete analysis of the *Quaestiones in tertium de anima* see F. Van Steenberghen, *Maître Siger de Brabant*, pp. 339-47.

[7] A detailed study of the text of the *De unitate intellectus* is an excellent theme for a seminar in medieval philosophy, as I have experienced first at Louvain, then at Milan and at Lublin (Poland). Everywhere this living and substantial text aroused great student interest.

In order to show this I need only recall that the anthropology of the Fathers of the Church, of Christian philosophers, and of theologians until the middle of the thirteenth century had always been *spiritualistic* and *dualistic*: spiritualistic, because the human soul is defined as a spiritual and immaterial reality and hence as immortal; dualistic, because man is thought of as a hybrid being, consisting of two substances, one corporeal and one spiritual. This dualistic view of human nature obviously comes from Plato. Dualism is normally heavily emphasized by non-Christian thinkers. Witness Plotinus among the Greeks, Avicenna in the Muslim world, and Avicebron among the Jews. In the Christian world, on the other hand, Platonic dualism is always more or less tempered due to the influence of Christianity, since the dogma of the Incarnation of the divine Word and that of redemption by Christ's death and resurrection imply that the Lord's body is really part of his human nature. This is confirmed once more by the dogma of resurrection of the flesh for all mankind. For St. Augustine, for instance, the body is no longer a "prison" for the soul as it is for Plato. Body and soul are two substances, but together they form human nature by their intimate union. In the thirteenth century still, in spite of the increasing influence of Aristotle, all Christian thinkers prior to Aquinas held a dualistic anthropology. This is true of St. Bonaventure, in spite of his undeniable efforts to safeguard the unity of the human person. And it is also true of Albert the Great, Thomas' teacher at Cologne.

Some have been misled in reading these forerunners of St. Thomas because of their usage of an Aristotelian terminology. But in fact their formulae never express the real Aristotelian doctrine of substantial union of soul and body in living beings when they speak of man.

Why did St. Thomas abandon this traditional anthropology? For two reasons, I believe. First of all, for one that is purely philosophical. The dualistic view does not do justice to the obvious unity of a human being, since a being that is truly one cannot consist of two substances. Secondly, for a reason based on expediency, which reinforced the first. Aristotle's philosophy held open the possibility of overcoming dualism by rigorous application to man of hylemorphic composition, that is to say, matter-form composition. On this basis it was possible to refute the Averroistic anthropology by showing that it cannot be reconciled with that of Aristotle. But defenders of the dualist anthropology, by basing themselves on a philosophy that was foreign to Aristotelianism, had no chance of winning acceptance from the Philosopher's dedicated followers or even of entering into meaningful dialogue with them.

Thomas Aquinas therefore introduced a new anthropology, with this as its fundamental thesis: *Man is a single substance, composed of matter and form. But this "substantial form" is entirely different in nature from that of lower forms, including animal souls. The human soul is an "immaterial" form and therefore "subsisting," and "incorruptible" or immortal.* As one can see, this fundamental thesis involves applying to man Aristotle's hylemorphic theory in fullest measure, while at the same time maintaining the immaterial and subsistent character of the soul. This position had never been defended before Aquinas.

Thomas did not merely state this new position. He proved it in rigorous fashion by showing that it is the only metaphysical explanation that can do justice to the data of consciousness. Let us now develop this fundamental thesis.

1. Man is *one substance*, that is to say, a subsistent being that is truly one. All the data provided by experience and especially by consciousness point to this substantial unity. I am conscious of being a "self," a single "conscious subject." I am also conscious of the fact that "my body" is a constituting element of my "self" and not a distinct and juxtaposed being with which I would only have more or less close relationships. All the activities that take place in this body are really mine: I breathe, I take nourishment, I have stomach trouble or liver trouble, I see, I understand, etc.

2. This substance is therefore the principle or *source of manifold activities* in differing degrees. The majority of these activities take place in a corporeal organ, but thinking and willing are immaterial in nature and hence "inorganic" activities. All of this, once more, is established by starting from experience and is expressed in a truly noteworthy doctrine on the activity and the capacity to expand of a finite substance. Due to this capacity this substance enters into contact with other finite substances and is thereby enriched.

3. This substance is a true *hylemorphic composite*. Once more, then, we are dealing with an interpretation required by the data of experience. In Aris-

totelianism one may demonstrate matter-form composition of corporeal substances in different but
converging ways. I will simply recall them here. One
may start from the fact of *substantial change*, which is
clear in the case of living beings since they are subject
to birth and death. One may also take as one's point
of departure the *passivity* that is involved in bodily
activity. One may start from the *continuous* change
that is found in bodies by reason of their quantity,
the distinctive characteristic of corporeal being, since
the body is defined in terms of extension. Finally, one
may start from the *multiplicity of individuals within the
same species*, a fact that is difficult to deny at least in
living beings which reproduce themselves within the
same species. But all of these signs pointing to matter-
form composition are found in man as well as in animals. Man is subject to birth and death. He is passive
in his organic activities. Such activities are subject to
time, the measure of continuous change. Finally, man
reproduces himself within the human species, which
includes countless individual men. None of these
facts could be accounted for if the human substance
were viewed as a "pure form," that is, as a simple
essence or substantial determination in the pure state.

4. But man's substantial form or human soul is
very *unusual in nature*, and this enables it to serve as
the meeting point between the world of the corporeal
and the purely spiritual. It is here that the originality
and, in my opinion, the genius of St. Thomas manifests itself. Again, we are not dealing with a mere
hypothesis, or a theory invented out of thin air to
solve a particular problem or to save a religious doctrine. It is rather a metaphysical conclusion required

by the data of consciousness. And it is here that Thomas both meets and overcomes the Averroist position.

The dominant fact that controls Thomas' metaphysical view of the human soul is, in brief, the *cogito*. I am conscious of thinking. "It is evident that this individual man thinks," writes Thomas in his *De unitate intellectus*. In other words, intellectual activity, which Aristotle had shown to be immaterial and inorganic, is truly an activity of the human individual that I am. Starting from this undeniable fact, St. Thomas demonstrates that the soul, the substantial principle of this activity, must be man's substantial form, even though it itself is immaterial in nature. In brief, then, it is at one and the same time the *form of matter* and an *immaterial form*.

—*form of matter*: it constitutes with the material principle the human substance, and the unique source of all of man's activities.

—*immaterial form*: that is to say, a form that is spiritual in nature, analogous to the separate forms of Aristotle or the pure spirits of Christian theology. As a consequence it is a *subsisting* form and, therefore, incorruptible, immortal, imperishable, even when the other composing principle, matter, is lacking due to the destruction of the human substance through death.

This fundamental thesis carries with it an important corollary. The human soul is directly created by God at the end of a biological process which leads to the production of a new human individual. It is because of his creationist metaphysics that Thomas was able to escape from the impasse in which Aristotle had found himself. As we have already indicated, the Stagirite could not conceive of the coming into being of an immaterial soul in the course of time, since for him every substance separated from matter was eternal and uncaused. For St. Thomas, on the contrary, as for all other Christian teachers, the coming into being of immaterial substances in the course of time does not present any great difficulty, since for them the creative influx is a permanent causality which gives being to all new entities that appear in the course of the universe's development. In thus accounting for the origin of the soul by creation St. Thomas' teaching does not differ from that of his Christian predecessors.

One can see how the anthropology of Thomas Aquinas meets and refutes the Averroist anthropology. The data of consciousness force one to recognize that the intellective soul is man's substantial form. Like all substantial forms it is individuated by its relationship to matter and can be multiplied numerically within its species, since God creates each soul in and for a determined body. The human soul is therefore not a "separate substance" in the Aristotelian sense and, as a consequence, need not be unique in its species, as the Averroists maintain. It truly is a "substantial form" while also being a "subsisting form."

Now we shall consider Thomas' reaction to Averroist monopsychism by turning to his *De unitate intellectus*. Within the limited confines of the University of Paris, and after Bonaventure's interventions of 1267 and 1268, Siger's more than temerarious teaching there could not have remained unknown, and all the more so since his was not an isolated case. Documents from that period point to the existence of a group of heterodox Masters who had gathered around him. Thomas Aquinas could not ignore the indignant protests raised by Bonaventure and one may be certain that, after his return to Paris, he discreetly informed himself about the frame of mind and the teaching of the Masters envisioned by Bonaventure. It would not have been difficult for Thomas while at Saint-Jacques, the Dominican House, to acquire the notes of students who were studying in the Faculty of Arts. He quickly recognized the gravity of the situation and among those mistaken positions then being circulated in that faculty, he judged especially dangerous Averroist monopsychism. His judgment was fully justified because, among all the heresies denounced by Bonaventure, none would have more disastrous consequences of a moral and religious nature than this position which would eliminate the personality, moral responsibility, and immortality of individual human beings.

Faithful to his mission to serve truth, Thomas began to prepare a brief treatise wherein he will systematically refute the Averroist position while restricting himself to the purely philosophical level. He is well aware of the sincere conviction which inspires the young Masters of Arts. Their fervor for Aristotle blinds them to such an extent that they fly in the face of common sense as well as of their Christian faith. In such a situation, exhortations and anathemas are of little effect. It is necessary rather to meet one's adversary on his own ground, which means, in the case at hand, to carry on the debate in the light of

Aristotelianism and purely philosophical principles.

Thomas' brief treatise was put into circulation in 1270, probably early in that year. It is known under the title *De unitate intellectus*, although certain manuscripts add to this *contra Averroistas* or *contra Averroistas Parisienses.* Codex 225 of Corpus Christi College, Oxford, includes this valuable colophon: *Haec scripsit Thomas* (ms. *taliter*) *contra magistrum Sigerum de Brabantia* (ms. *Barbantia*) *et alios plurimos Parisius in philosophia regentes anno Domini 1270.* Consultation of Thomas' treatise reveals many interesting points.

First of all, his exposition envisions primarily the teaching of Averroes himself, who is often named and whose positions are discussed. On the other hand, in many passages Thomas speaks of his adversaries in the plural and here clearly has in mind Latin followers of the Commentator (Averroes). Finally, he also attacks a particular Master whom he does not name. This appears first in a passage where he seems to have in mind a particular adversary: *Quaerendum est autem ab eo qui hoc ponit, primo, quid sit hoc singulare quod est Socrates. . . . Et quantum ex sua positione videtur, hoc tertium accipiet.* But it should be noted that Thomas then immediately changes to the plural: *Procedamus ergo contra eos. . . .* But this reference to a particular adversary is most evident in the treatise's epilogue (§122-124), where Thomas indignantly denounces the intolerable attitude of a Master who, all the while declaring himself to be Christian, defends positions which are absolutely incompatible with Christian faith. Here he repeats literally certain statements by that Master, but his source for these has not yet been found.

However, it does not seem that in this treatise Thomas uses published works of the Averroist Masters. First of all, certain passages betray some hesitation on his part concerning positions defended by his adversaries. Thomas does not seem to have certain and precise knowledge of their positions. Moreover, in the closing lines of his treatise Thomas reproaches his opponent for not exposing his positions to criticism by the learned public: "Let him not speak in corners nor in the presence of young boys (*coram pueris*), who do not know how to pass judgment concerning such difficult matters. But let him reply in writing to this treatise, if he dares."

How is one to reconcile all of this with the literal citations offered by Thomas in the epilogue? The problem disappears if one acknowledges that he used *reportationes* of Siger's course or of those of other Averroist Masters. While citing the scandalous positions collected in these *reportationes*, he can also denounce the clandestine character of the teaching which they echo.

It is generally agreed that the epilogue of the *De unitate intellectus* has in mind Siger of Brabant, as the colophon from the Oxford codex suggests. However, the remarks which are offensive to Christianity and which Thomas cites are not to be found in the *reportatio* of Siger's *Quaestiones in tertium de anima* which has come down to us. These citations could be taken from a more complete *reportatio* of the same lectures, or else from another of Siger's courses. In any event, it is difficult to establish with certainty that the author of the *De unitate* had knowledge of the *Quaestiones in tertium de anima*. All that one can say is that many positions defended in this *reportatio* are opposed by Thomas in his opusculum: man is a complex being resulting from the union of the unique intellect with a vegetative-sensitive soul which informs a body; the intellect is united to the body as its mover, not as its substantial form, even though this union is closer than that between celestial movers and that which they move; Siger treats at length of hell-fire; finally, he has direct knowledge of no other Peripatetics apart from Averroes and Avicenna. Nonetheless, the similarity between Siger's *reportatio* and Thomas' opusculum is never sufficiently great for one to be certain that there is direct literary or textual inter-dependence.

Since it is morally certain that Siger of Brabant is the Master envisioned by the epilogue of the *De unitate*, this page, which is one of the few in which Thomas gives vent to his personal feelings, is at the same time quite revealing with respect to Siger's personal dispositions before 1270. He speaks of the "Latins" and of "their Law" (religion) as if he were alien to them. He doubts that monopsychism is opposed to Christian faith. He qualifies as a "position" the teaching of the faith. He says that God himself could not multiply the human intellect, since such would entail contradiction. While affirming that unicity of the intellect is a necessary conclusion established by human reason, he claims to hold the opposite position as a believer. This implies that the faith has for its object that which is false and impossible, since it contradicts that which is necessarily true. He presumes to discuss problems which do not pertain to philosophy, but only to faith, such as seeking to determine how the separated soul can suffer from the fire of hell. Here he rejects the views of the theologians. Finally, he circulates his ideas in secret places (literally: in corners) and before young boys. These criticisms fully correspond to the rationalist and audacious attitude of the *Quaestiones in tertium de anima.*

Thomas' anti-Averroistic treatise is of unusual philosophical density, and detailed study of the same would require lengthy discussion. Here I shall limit myself to the essentials: a summary analysis, and some reflections on the author's doctrinal position.[8]

The *De unitate intellectus* includes an introduction (§1-2), the corpus of the treatise (§ 3-123), and a brief conclusion (§ 124). The corpus of this work is divided into five chapters in the oldest manuscripts, and this division probably goes back to St. Thomas himself. But the work's structure is more complex. This becomes evident from a careful reading of the text, since the author indicates by very clear transition phrases the organization of his exposition. Thomas distinguishes two fundamental aspects in the Averroist position concerning the human intellect: the intellect is *not the substantial form* of the body; and not being its substantial form, the intellect cannot be multiplied in individuals, but is *unique* for the entire hu-

---

[8] L. W. Keeler published in 1936 a very good and almost critical edition of this treatise: *Sancti Thomae Aquinatis tractatus de unitate intellectus.* Earlier editions are not to be used. See F. Van Steenberghen, *La philosophie au XIIIe siècle*, Philosophes médiévaux IX (Louvain-Paris, 1966), p. 432, n. 36. The *De unitate intellectus* has recently appeared in the Leonine edition (v. 43, pp. 243-314, 1976), but I shall cite from the Keeler edition for the reader's convenience. Also cf. F. Van Steenberghen, "Corrections au texte du *De unitate intellectus* de Thomas d'Aquin," *Bulletin de philosophie médiévale* 19 (1977), pp. 65-67.

man race. These two mistaken positions on Averroes' part give rise to the general division of Thomas' treatise.

The *Prooemium* supplies some indications concerning the origins and the extent of the Averroist movement (§1, 6-7), alludes to Thomas' earlier writings against the teaching of Averroes (§1, 12-13), and indicates that the present exposition is to be purely philosophical, based on a critical exegesis of Aristotle (§2, 17-31).

The first part of the body or corpus (cc. I-III, §3-85) includes an exegetical section (cc. I-II) and a philosophical section (c. III). In the exegetical section Thomas first undertakes to interpret the major passages of Aristotle's *De anima* where his teaching on the intellect is presented. And he attempts to show by skillful commentary that Aristotle's text excludes the Averroist interpretation (§ 3-26). In support of his reading of the *De anima* he cites a text from the *Physics* in order to present more precisely the Aristotelian view of hierarchy of forms. The human soul is the highest of the forms united to matter, since it has a power of operation, the intellect, which is not joined to a corporeal organ. It is in this sense that the intellect is said to be "separate," and not in Averroes' meaning, who would make of it a separate substance (§ 27-30). Continuing his exegesis of Aristotle, Thomas rejects the arguments drawn by the Averroists from the immortality of the intellect (§ 31-43), and then those that they base on the intellect's origin (§ 44-50).

This explanation of Aristotle's texts is followed by a complementary investigation (c. II) of the Greek

(§ 51-56) and Arabic (§ 57-58) Peripatetic school. Thomas shows that Themistius, Theophrastus, and Alexander of Aphrodisias among the Greeks, and Avicenna and Algazel among the Arabs viewed the intellect as a power of the soul, not as a separate substance. He dwells with satisfaction on Themistius' commentary and reproduces lengthy passages therefrom. He was the first to make use of the recent translation of this work by William of Moerbeke, and is evidently delighted to oppose the authentic Themistius to that presented by Averroes' commentary. This lengthy exegetical section ends with a celebrated conclusion (§ 59) where Aquinas condemns the Aristotelianism of Averroes, "who was not so much a Peripatetic as a corruptor of Peripatetic philosophy" (*quam philosophiae peripateticae depravator*).

The philosophical section of the first part (c. III) includes an exposition of arguments whereby one can show that the intellective soul is man's substantial form (§ 60-82), and then a refutation of the objections formulated by the Averroists (§ 83-85). The positive exposition dwells at length on the basic argument, taken from Aristotle, which turns on an undeniable datum of consciousness (§ 62, 22): *hic homo singularis intelligit* ("This individual man understands"). Thomas shows that neither Averroes' explanation (§ 63-66) nor that offered by certain Averroists (§ 67-79) can account for this inescapable fact. After this major argument, which is of a *psychological* nature, come two complementary arguments: one based on considerations of a *logical* nature concerning the human species (§ 80); and one based on exigencies pertaining to the *moral* order (§ 81-82). His critique of the Averroist objections serves as an occasion for Thomas to identify the human soul as a form of matter (*forma materiae*), but not a material form (*forma materialis*). Hence it falls between purely material forms and separate forms (§ 83-85).

The second part of the corpus (cc. IV-V, § 86-123) takes up the second aspect of the Averroistic position: unicity of the intellect for all mankind. After indicating the exact subject of the debate (§ 86), Thomas divides his exposition into two sections, one positive and one negative. In the first he attempts to show that unicity of the possible intellect raises insurmountable difficulties (§ 87-98). And in the second he refutes the objections raised by the Averroists (c. V, § 99-123).

Unicity of the intellect leads to absurd consequences (§ 87-91). Only one man would exist (§87, 21-25), or at least only one intelligent being in all of humanity (§ 89, 62-63). Consequently, only one being would enjoy a will (§ 89, 63-73). Finally, there could only be one act of understanding with respect to one and the same object (§ 90-91). All of these consequences run counter to human experience. But unicity of the intellect is also incompatible with Aristotle's teaching, and here Thomas completes the exegesis which he had presented in the first part (§ 92-98).

The objections considered by Thomas are five in number. The first includes, in addition to the major difficulty, a secondary one which the Averroists present as following from the first one (§ 99-105). Thomas' discussion of this fundamental objection is one of the high points of his treatise. It is here that one also finds a passage which has already given rise to extended controversy between different interpreters of Aquinas (see: *Valde autem ruditer*). After this twofold objection bearing on the nature of the intellective *soul*, another objection, based on the nature of intellectual *activity*, affords Thomas the opportunity of presenting a remarkable exposition on the realism of human knowledge and on the way knowledge is communicated to others (§ 106-113). The third objection is based on the finality of spiritual substances (§ 114-116). The fourth, joined with the hypothesis of eternity of the world and of species, attempts to show that if the intellective soul were multiplied numerically as are individual human beings, this would result in an infinity of separated souls, which is rejected as impossible (§ 117-118). The last objection, which appeals to the authority of the Greek and Arabic Peripatetics, is turned against the Averroists. Algazel and Avicenna, Themistius, Theophrastus, Aristotle and even Plato himself, all admitted of a plurality of human intellects. Once more Thomas comments that Averroes should be referred to as a "corruptor of Peripatetic philosophy" (§ 119-121).

Thomas immediately extends his attack against Averroes to the Latin Averroists and especially to one of those, who remains unnamed, but from whom Thomas reproduces in order to stigmatize certain daring remarks which can only be regarded as revolting when uttered by a Christian (§ 122-123).

In his treatise's brief conclusion Thomas recalls that he has refuted Averroism according to strictly philosophical procedures, without basing his case on the authority of faith. He then hurls a challenge at his foes and invites them to reply to him, if they dare, rather than circulate their views in secret and before young boys who are incapable of critically evaluating such difficult problems. And he promises that they will encounter stiff opposition from many defenders of truth (§ 124).

This violent reaction to which the *De unitate* bears witness is to be accounted for, undoubtedly, by the grave threat which Averroism posed for Christian faith. But it also betrays on Thomas' part a desire to dispute with Averroes his claim to be a follower of Aristotle, whom he had compromised, and to preserve for Christian thought the essentials of the Peripatetic legacy.

What is one to say of Thomas' exegesis of Aristotle in comparison with that of Averroes? A detailed investigation would be required in order for one to reply adequately to this question. But in the main, one may say this. Averroes draws the consequences which are logically implied by Aristotle's metaphysics when one tries to resolve the problem of the nature of the intellect. Thomas bases his case on psychological analyses and on empirical data offered by Aristotle with respect to intellectual activity, and shows that these data and analyses imply his (Thomas') view of the intellect. Each exploits those texts which support his interpretation. Each leaves to the side those which create difficulties for him. And each interprets obscure passages in a way which supports his position. The literal commentary on the texts from Aristotle in the *De unitate intellectus* is usually faithful and quite penetrating. But it imposes on Aristotle, in an ingenious and persuasive manner, an impeccable logical consistency in the development of his ideas and the acceptance of the consequences of his statements, all the while leaving to the side the difficulties which this "Thomistic" interpretation raises within the general framework of his system. Averroes does the same thing, but in the opposite direction.

For example, let us compare the two with respect to one passage from the *De anima*.[9] In saying that the intellect is a "perpetual" reality, Aristotle undoubtedly opposes it before all else to other "parts" of the soul, which are corruptible. But in stating that the intellect is incorruptible, he recognizes that its existence is not tied to that of the body and of other "parts" of the soul. But he does not say anything here about the ontological status of the intellect. Averroes and Thomas agree that, for Aristotle, the intellect survives the death of the individual human being. But within the framework of the Stagirite's metaphysics, a perpetual and immaterial reality — which is separable from the body — can only be a separate substance. Averroes says as much. Thomas avoids taking this step.

To what degree does the *De unitate intellectus* successfully meet the difficulties raised by Averroism in connection with a metaphysical study of the problem of man?

In this discussion a number of points are held in common by both parties: divine causality, the universal source of being; the doctrine of potency and act with its diverse applications; the hylemorphic theory in its original purity; the distinction between sub-

---

[9] See Aristotle, *De anima* II, c. 2 (413b 26-27); Averroes, *De anima*, II, comm. 21; Thomas Aquinas, *De unitate intellectus*, §8-9.

stance and accidents; and Aristotle's physics. And as regards the problem of man, Thomas and the Averroists accept the biological views of the Stagirite, the existence in man of a soul which is the substantial form of the body, the immateriality of the intellect and its transcendence with respect to corporeal activities, the existence of an agent intellect, and the doctrine of abstraction. The debate is clearly circumscribed, therefore. It has to do with determining the *nature of the intellect* or of the principle of intellectual activity, its exact relationship with individual human beings, and as a consequence, its multiplication in individuals, its origin, and its future destiny..

Within Aristotle's philosophy an immaterial substance is one which escapes from the conditions of matter and the vicissitudes of cosmic evolution. It can only be eternal, unbegotten, and incorruptible. How could it *begin* to be at a given moment in time, since it cannot result from natural generation? Hence, if the *nous* is an immaterial substance, how could it begin to exist at the moment when an individual human being begins his earthly career as the result of a biological process of procreation? And if it preexists as a separate substance, how can it serve as the substantial form of matter and be multiplied numerically as are material forms? It is easy to understand why Aristotle remains silent with respect to these problems.

At first glance, Averroes and the Latin Averroists have at their disposition a new and extremely important element for the solution of these difficulties, since they recognize God's creative causality. One would think, therefore, that the idea of a spiritual soul which is called into existence by creation at the

moment when a new biological individual member of
the human species comes into being would not be
inaccessible to them. This solution completely escapes
them, however, for reasons which must be identified
in each particular case, but which may be traced back
to the following. On the one hand, their excessive
reliance on the Aristotelian framework leads them to
accept without reservation a dualistic view of the
universe which sharply opposes the world of spiritual
substances and that of corporeal substances. On the
other hand and especially, serious weaknesses in their
understanding of creative causality prevent them
from adopting the solution of Thomas Aquinas. For
them every immediate effect of the First Cause is
eternal and unchangeable. All "novelty" in reality
is to be explained by the development proper to the
material universe. The appearance of new immaterial
substances is no more conceivable here than in the
original Aristotelianism. Thus the Averroists find
themselves being carried along the same path as Aristotle himself, and this in spite of the superiority of
their metaphysics to that of the Philosopher.

When one examines Thomas' reaction in his *De
unitate intellectus*, one is surprised to observe that he
never raises the problem explicitly from the standpoint of creative causality and does not directly criticize the weaknesses of his adversaries with respect to
this. Did he not grasp this important aspect of the
issue? Or was he poorly informed about the metaphysical principles of Siger and his group so as not
to appreciate the crux of their difficulties. Perhaps.
But another explanation seems to be more likely.
Thomas was well aware of the weaknesses of Aristo-

telianism in metaphysics. Being deeply concerned with preserving Peripatetic thought in its essential insights and to correct it where necessary, it may be that he chose not to conduct the debate on the metaphysical level so as to avoid presenting Aristotle in a bad light, an Aristotle who was already sufficiently compromised by Averroes.

Be that as it may, Thomas Aquinas adopts another method, or if you will, another tactic in his battle against Averroism. He poses the problem of the intellect on the level of psychological experience. "For it is evident that this individual man understands. We would never inquire concerning the intellect unless we understood" (§ 62, 21-23). Starting from this undeniable datum of consciousness, he establishes with all the logical rigor of Aristotelian principles that the intellect is an operative power whose substantial principle is, to be sure, an immaterial reality, but at the same time man's substantial form. This principle is the intellective or human soul, the unique source of all of man's operations. A form *of matter*, the human soul is not a *material form*. It is not precontained within the potentialities of matter and its appearance cannot be explained, even on the level of second causes, by the laws of cosmic evolution. It is created by God at the term of the generation of man. As a form *of matter*, the human soul is individuated by its relationship to this determined matter, since this relationship is essential to its constitution. For the human soul is created as the substantial form of this given human organism. Consequently, it is no more difficult to account for a multiplicity of human souls within the human species than it is to account for multiplicity of other substantial forms. A form *of matter*, the human soul is also an *immaterial* form, which intrinsically transcends the material order. Being capable of inorganic operation, it can subsist without its body, since operation is an expression of being. Man subsists, to be sure, but the human soul subsists in man and accounts for the fact that the human composite subsists. Finally, being a subsistent form and independent from the conditions of matter, the human soul does not cease to subsist when the human organism is corrupted. The human soul survives destruction of the composite and lives on in terms of its reality, its individuality, and its activity, granted that the conditions for its activity are greatly modified in its separated state.

Such is, in the main, the solution proposed by the *De unitate* to the problem of the intellective soul. Its argumentation is irrefutable for any Aristotelian who accepts the initial datum: "This individual man understands." The Averroists will soon have to take this into account. But the *De unitate*'s influence would have surely been more decisive if its author had discussed in greater depth the metaphysical difficulties which were troubling the Averroists and which may be reduced to this fundamental question: How can a spiritual and subsistent form be at one and the same time the substantial form of a body? The objection is clearly formulated in the *De unitate*. It is not accidental to a substantial form to be united to matter, but its relationship to matter is *essential*. Consequently, if the body is corrupted, the soul which is its substantial form must also disappear with it.[10] In other words,

---

[10] *De unitate intellectus*, §32. The difficulty reappears under other forms farther on in the work. See §83-84 and §99-100.

the substantial form is *essentially* a co-principle and therefore cannot even be conceived without its correlative principle. A substantial form is intrinsically constituted by its relationship to matter, and it is in its union with such determined matter that it finds the reason for its subsistence and its individuality. In a word, the Averroists do not admit of any possible intermediary between a material form and a subsisting form, between a form which is a principle of being and a form which is a complete and immaterial substance.

In order to resolve this formulation of the problem Thomas once more falls back upon the solid ground of psychological experience and, from an analysis of certain vital activities, concludes to the existence of two kinds of hylemorphic composites. In the first type it is the composite which subsists and the form is nothing but a principle *by which* the composite subsists (*huiusmodi formae ipsae quidem proprie loquendo non sunt, sed eis aliquid est* [§ 37, 76-78]). In the second type, that is to say, in human composites, it is the form which possesses being (or subsistence) and the composite which subsists by reason of the form (*ipsa est quae habet esse, nec est per esse compositi tantum, sicut aliae formae, sed magis compositum est per esse eius* [§ 38]). From this it follows that the human soul can subsist without its body. It can, therefore, be found successively under the condition of a substantial form and under that of a separated form.

In light of these explanations, Thomas now judges himself to be in position to reply briefly to the difficulty raised above. It is *essential* to the soul to be united to the body, he says, but this union is impeded

65

per accidens when the body dissolves and disappears (§ 43, 138-40). One would expect from him some explanation for this surprising statement, but an example taken from Aristotelian physics is offered instead: ". . . just as it pertains *per se* to a light thing to be up . . . yet it may happen because of some hindrance that it is not up" (§ 43, 140-143). However, a comparison is not an argument. He should have shown in what sense it is no more "essential" to the soul for it to be united to the body than it is to a light body for it to occupy its natural place. In order to do this it would be necessary for him to distinguish between the original constitution of the soul in its status as a substantial form at the terminus of human generation and its subsequent existence. It is *essential* to the human soul for it to *be created in a body and for a body* at the terminus of generation. Without this it would not be a substantial form but an angelic form and therefore subsistent and unique in its species. It is *not essential* for this same soul to *remain united* to the body because, once it has been constituted in its reality and its individuality, since it can subsist alone it no longer depends essentially on its co-principle. In brief, here Thomas should have taken up the theme of creation of the soul. Without this the existence of a form which is both substantial and subsistent is inconceivable. He did not do this, for reasons which remain unknown to us.[11] Perhaps, as I have suggested, he did not wish to shift the debate to the level of creative causality, where Aristotle's position is so

---

[11] St. Thomas had discussed this question in earlier works. See for instance, *De potentia*, q. 3, aa. 9-11.

weak. But it may be that neither Thomas nor his adversaries clearly recognized that the heart of the difficulty and the fundamental reason for their disagreement was to be found at this level. The hindsight afforded by history enables us to see more clearly the conditions of the controversy.[12]

III

In the third part of this lecture I would like to attempt to reply briefly to two questions: 1) By his anthropology has Thomas Aquinas adequately resolved the difficulties raised by the Averroists? 2) Is his anthropology still satisfying for twentieth-century man?

As regards the first question one could reply by studying the Averroist writings subsequent to Thomas' *De unitate intellectus* which are more or less directly replies to that treatise. Let us limit ourselves to one example, which tells much about the reaction of an intelligent Averroist: Siger of Brabant's remarkable little treatise *De anima intellectiva*, written ca. 1273 and, therefore, approximately three years after Thomas' work.[13]

Clearly Siger was not convinced by the argumentation whereby Thomas had wished to prove that the intellective soul is man's substantial form. Siger is unable to admit that an immaterial soul is substantially united to matter. That would be to reduce it to

---

[12] For more complete analysis of the *De unitate intellectus* see F. Van Steenberghen, *Maître Siger de Brabant,* pp. 347-60.

[13] See B. Bazán, *Siger de Brabant. Quaestiones in tertium de anima. De anima intellectiva. De aeternitate mundi*, pp. 70-112. For the discussion on the nature of the soul see ch. III, pp. 77-88.

the level of a material form, and this would lead to two unacceptable consequences. Abstract intellectual knowledge would become impossible, and the immortality of the soul would be compromised since a material form is essentially united to matter and disappears when the composite is destroyed.

However, St. Thomas had stressed that a form *of matter* is not necessarily a *material* form which would lack any subsistence of its own. And he had avoided the two consequences drawn by Siger. He avoided the first, according to which abstract intellectual knowledge would be impossible, by distinguishing between the soul and its power of operation. The soul is the form of the body and therefore immediately united to matter, but its power of operation, the intellect, is an inorganic power, that is to say, a power that operates without a corporeal organ. It can, therefore, receive abstract and universal ideas. To the second difficulty, the alleged denial of immortality, he had replied in advance by conceding that it is essential to a substantial form to be united to matter, but that this union can be impeded in accidental fashion (*per accidens*) by reason of the body's disappearance. And he had justified this possibility by the comparison taken from Aristotelian physics. It is essential for a light body to be up, that is to say, in its "natural place," but it may happen that such a body is held down by some obstacle.

Siger does not find these explanations acceptable. To the first he replies that a power of operation cannot be more immaterial than that substance from which it flows. He does not reply expressly to the second, but one can be certain that he would not accept this comparison, and one can understand why. For a light body to "be up" is clearly a property that follows from its essence (according to the ancient physics), but it is a property of an accidental nature that can be countered in a "violent" manner by an external obstacle. But to "be united with matter" appears to be the very essence of a substantial form.

What is one to say of these replies? The first is not well grounded, for St. Thomas had explicitly dealt with this difficulty: "If one should object," he says, "that a power of the soul cannot be more immaterial or more simple than the soul's essence, this objection would hold if the human soul were a simple material form, and totally dependent on matter. But the human soul possesses its own being and the dignity of this form transcends the capacity of matter" (*De unitate intellectus*, §84). In other words, St. Thomas accepts without reservation the principle on which the objection rests. An operative power cannot be more perfect than the substance from which it emanates, according to the well known axiom: *agere sequitur formam* ("action is proportioned to substantial form").

As regards Siger's second reply, it deserves more attention, for the analogy with a light body was certainly inadequate, as I have just shown. In my opinion Thomas should have formulated his reply differently and said that it is not essential to the human soul to be *united to matter*, but it is essential to it to be *created in matter* and for matter. In other words, in order to justify the status of a soul which is the *form of matter* without being a *material form*, one must appeal to the notion of creation. The human soul must be created for a determined body and be individuated by its essential relation to that body. Without this it would be a separate substance, a pure spirit. But it is created as an immaterial and subsistent form. Without this it would be a purely material and corruptible form.

This doctrine of the creation of the human soul is in perfect conformity with St. Thomas' thought and is presented in many of his writings. It is clearly presupposed and even hinted at in many passages in his *De unitate intellectus*, but this theme of creation of the soul is never explicitly introduced there, and this may be the major reason for Siger's resistance to that work.

Let us now consider the second question: Is Thomas' anthropology still satisfying today?

A first remark is obvious. His anthropology is primarily a *metaphysical* or *ontological* interpretation of human nature. Hence it is without meaning or value for those who reject metaphysical knowledge as a mere intellectual game, a mental construction without meaning. I cannot here enter into a discussion of the nature and value of metaphysics. Personally, I am well aware of the limits and the difficulties of metaempirical knowledge. I am also convinced of its rich possibilities, and of the value of its methods and conclusions. If one takes this as given, then what is one to think of Thomas Aquinas' understanding of human nature?

In my opinion this view answers perfectly to the data of psychological experience and, to my knowledge, no better interpretation has been proposed since the thirteenth century. But this does not mean that the Thomistic anthropology was definitively and perfectly worked out in the thirteenth century. It can and should be perfected and developed in many directions, and I would like to suggest some ways in which this should be done.

1. *The demonstration of the spirituality of the soul.* St. Thomas is, perhaps, too dependent on Aristotle on this point. Certain characteristics of thinking, overlooked by the Stagirite, reveal more clearly than those he has used that this activity is not, in itself, organic in nature. For instance, my knowledge of the past as past, of the future as future, of the absent as absent. I think of Kant as a person who lived in the eighteenth century. I speak of the world's population in the year 2000. I "represent" to myself Pope Paul VI, but I know that he is in Rome, three thousand miles from here. It is absolutely impossible for one to account for these facts by appealing to purely organic knowledge.

2. *The demonstration of the soul's immortality.* Many psychologists today reject the notion of the soul's survival while insisting that all of our activities, even the noblest, are conditioned by the state of our organism. Thus a brain lesion may interfere with our intellectual activity and even put an end to our conscious life. This is an evident fact, and one of which Thomas was well aware. He taught not only that we are unable to know intellectually without the aid of sense and imagination, but that even after we have acquired ideas, we cannot make use of them without the concurrence of images. Even more, we cannot formulate a perfect judgment, bearing on reality, without the concurrence of sense experience (ST, *Prima Pars*, q. 84, aa. 7, 8). But according to him these are conditions required for human thinking

71

which result from the union of the soul with the body. This does not prevent the soul, as an immaterial and subsistent form, from being capable of surviving the death of the human composite. It will then begin a new life in its state as a "separated soul" and will have a natural activity suitable for that state.

It will undoubtedly be possible to establish with greater force the immortality of the soul as necessarily following from its spiritual nature. But one may also find confirmation for this thesis in the doctrine (even the philosophical doctrine) of divine Providence. The wisdom, justice, and goodness of the Creator require that *personal* creatures, being both conscious and responsible and having an end in and for themselves, enjoy an imperishable existence. These same divine perfections also require that the moral order be respected, that good and evil, obviously not receiving their just deserts here below, receive them in the life to come.

3. *In many places in his writings St. Thomas describes the nature of the human soul in rather strange language*, at least at first sight. In matter-form composites below man, he says, being (*esse*) pertains to the composite alone, while the composing principles (matter and form) exist only by reason of the being of the composite. But in the case of man, being first pertains to the soul, while the composite "participates" in the being of the soul. This teaching surely expresses in striking fashion the unusual status of the human soul among substantial forms. But one could get the impression that it was only a case of special pleading. There is need, therefore, to present the meaning of this teaching more precisely and to show that

it is indeed *demanded* by the empirical data which ground his anthropology.

4. Thomists today are faced with a great task: the *confrontation of their anthropology with the findings of the human sciences*, especially of positive psychology. Since St. Thomas' doctrine claims to be a rigorous metaphysical interpretation of psychological experience, there is good reason to believe that this confrontation will make manifest the perfect harmony of these two regions of human knowing.

5. Finally, considerable effort should be made in order to express correctly St. Thomas' anthropology. This requires some explanation. I mentioned above that Thomas' predecessors made use of an Aristotelian terminology in order to formulate their dualistic anthropology, the latter being inspired by Plato and St. Augustine. And I have observed that this terminology could give rise to inaccurate interpretations. We find ourselves faced with a similar situation in the case of St. Thomas, but in the opposite direction. He often expresses his Aristotelian anthropology in dualistic terms. Such happens whenever he refers to the soul as the "form of the body" (*forma corporis*), whereas one should rather speak of the "form of matter" (*forma materiae*). For the body is that concrete, extended reality that we perceive through the senses. It is not to the body but to prime matter that the soul is united as substantial form. It should also be noted here that almost all of Christian literature in the fields of theology, morality, and spirituality is dualistic in its language and often in its thought. This is unfortunate since such language is inaccurate and fails to correspond to the conclusions

of the human sciences. Thomists should, therefore, strive to correct these dualistic expressions in the writings of the Angelic Doctor. This is an important task if one wishes to bring out the value of the remarkable doctrine that serves as the foundation of his anthropology.

THE THIRD LECTURE

RATIONALISM

I

Until the end of the twelfth century the organization of studies in the Christian world was dominated by the Augustinian conception of "Christian Wisdom" as St. Augustine himself had presented it in his *De doctrina christiana.* According to this view all areas of profane knowledge were to be placed at the service of sacred science, that is, theology or the scientific study of divine revelation accepted on faith. This is the reason why the schools of liberal arts were viewed as preparatory schools, providing a general formation that was indispensable for those entering the advanced fields of study: theology, law or medicine. Philosophy was almost completely missing from this organization of studies, since, of all the philosophical disciplines known in the ancient world, only logic held a place in the program of the schools of liberal arts. Furthermore, since law and medicine were directed toward professional and practical ends, theology alone offered a scientific view of the universe, its origin and its destiny. In short, the Christian view of the world dominated, without competition, the intellectual life of the period.

This situation changed rapidly from the start of the thirteenth century. Translations from Arabic to Latin and from Greek to Latin introduced into the Christian world a vast amount of non-Christian literature, among which the writings of Aristotle held a preeminent place. These Aristotelian writings were accompanied at first by Arabic commentaries, and somewhat later by Greek ones. As I have already indicated in my preceding lectures, Aristotle's intellectual achievement made a deep impression on the Latin Masters. For them his work was the revelation of a scientific encyclopedia unknown until that time. The Philosopher now presented himself to them with all the prestige of a man of universal knowledge and an imposing view of the cosmos.

It was not long before the earlier structure of the Arts Faculty at Paris began to change. The *logica nova* (that part of the *Organon* or of Aristotle's logical treatises which had remained unknown until then) was introduced there, and then the *Ethics*. After lengthy resistance on the part of Church authorities, all the known writings of the Stagirite were given a place in the program of studies of that Faculty by a decree of March 19, 1255. This list even included three pseudo-Aristotelian (i.e., inauthentic) works, the *De causis*, the *De plantis*, and the *De differentia spiritus et animae*. From that time forward the Faculty of Arts had become in fact a philosophy faculty. And Aristotle's philosophy was taught there in its entirety.

It is clear that this new situation carried with it a serious danger for the unity of Christian thought, or if one prefers, the threat of rationalism. For the Masters in the Faculty of Arts began to attach ever greater importance to their vocation as philosophers, and their admiration for Aristotle continued to grow. Yet Greek and Arabic philosophy was, in many areas, in open contradiction with Christian thought. The Philosopher defended eternity of the world and of every species, including the human race. His anthropology was obscure on many points, and Averroes, the Commentator *par excellence*, had interpreted him as defending monopsychism, which would destroy the personality, responsibility, and immortality of human individuals. His ethics did not know of man's ultimate end in the life hereafter. Avicenna had defended a Neoplatonic metaphysics of emanation which included creation and providential care of the world through intermediary entities. Finally, many non-Christian philosophical teachings carried with them a decidedly deterministic accent.

Thus the Christian Masters in the Arts Faculty were soon faced with two profoundly different views of the universe. It was almost inevitable that some would come to the point of preferring the non-Christian view and of adopting a rationalistic and naturalistic vision of the universe. If this attitude developed, it would bring with it the threat of Neopaganism and would cause a tragic split within the intellectual unity of Christianity. All of the great theologians of the thirteenth century were aware of this danger, and each reacted in the way that appeared to him to be the most suitable or most demanded by the urgency of the situation. This is true of Bonaventure, Albert the Great, Roger Bacon, Thomas Aquinas, and later on, Raymond Lull.[1]

II

With this general picture of the "crisis" of the thirteenth century before us, we must now ask our-

---

[1] On the crisis of the thirteenth century see F. Van Steenberghen, *Aristotle in the West*, pp. 59-146 and 198-208.

selves some more precise questions. Are there in fact any signs of a rationalist current in the thirteenth century? When and under what forms did it appear? Was Thomas Aquinas aware of this rationalist thrust during his final sojourn in Paris, that is, from 1269 until 1272?

Let us note immediately that we possess very little *direct* evidence of such a current of rationalism before the Condemnation of December 10, 1270. That is to say, we have very few documents in which any Masters from the Arts Faculty betray a rationalist mentality. Before examining these direct indications, however, let us first pause and consider some *indirect* signs pointing to this rationalist tendency. The first of our indirect witnesses is St. Bonaventure, who in 1257 became Minister General (General Superior) of the Franciscans. In 1267 and 1268 he preached the Lenten sermons at the Franciscan church in Paris. Now these sermons show for the first time the existence of rationalist tendencies in the Arts Faculty. Let us examine them more closely.

In 1267 Bonaventure took as his theme the ten commandments (*De decem praeceptis*). In these sermons he denounces the threat which was growing in the ranks of the Arts Faculty. He condemns many heretical doctrines being taught there, and offers as the first reason for these doctrinal deviations "the improper use of philosophical inquiry." In conclusion he exhorts his listeners to remain faithful to the teachings of Christian revelation. Now what is this "improper use of philosophical inquiry?" The historical context allows us to account for the great Franciscan preacher's judgment in the following way.

Captivated by the philosophy of Aristotle, certain Masters of Arts lost sight of the role and place of philosophy in the ensemble of Christian wisdom. They regarded philosophy as an independent knowledge and pursued it without any concern for Christian orthodoxy. The sermons *De decem praeceptis* permit us to state that certain heretical teachings were already being circulated early in 1267.

In the following year, 1268, Bonaventure preached on the *Gifts of the Holy Spirit* (*De donis Spiritus Sancti*) and once again he condemned various doctrines from non-Christian philosophy. In his fourth sermon, devoted to the gift of knowledge, he places his audience on guard against rationalism. For the Christian, he states, philosophy can only be a stage in the search for complete truth, since it cannot provide an adequate solution to problems concerning man's destiny. He who stops with philosophy as sufficient wisdom falls into the shadows of darkness. Now this is precisely the blind route pursued by the rationalist when he disregards the higher light of divine revelation.[2]

Bonaventure, however, is not the only witness to this situation. There is no doubt that from the moment of his return to Paris in January, 1269, Thomas Aquinas was informed about the dangerous situation in the Faculty of Arts. He quickly recognized the seriousness of the errors that certain Masters were teaching there. He was especially struck by one particularly dangerous doctrine, Averroist monopsychism. As we have already seen, he published his cele-

---

[2] On Bonaventure's interventions in 1267 and 1268 see F. Van Steenberghen, *Maître Siger de Brabant*, pp. 33-46.

brated *De unitate intellectus* early in 1270. On the last page of that treatise Thomas clearly denounces the rationalist attitude of a certain Master, who, while not named, is almost certainly Siger of Brabant. Reference has been made to a colophon or note in an Oxford manuscript of this work indicating that it was written against Siger and other Regent Masters at Paris in the year 1270.[3]

As we have also seen above, in this final page Thomas seems to be citing textually from a document he had before his eyes. The author of this document speaks of "Latins" and "Catholics" as though he were not one of them. "The Latins," he tells us, "do not admit the thesis of monopsychism because their law *perhaps* teaches the contrary." Or again, "this is the reason why Catholics seem to hold their position." The same author then declares that *by using reason* he *necessarily* concludes that the intellect is unique. Yet he firmly holds the opposed position because of *faith*. Finally, he dares dispute about matters which are not proper to the domain of philosophy, but belong rather to the realm of pure faith. For example, he discusses the fire of hell, and says that the teachings of the theologians with respect to this are to be rejected.[4]

Such strong statements indicate very clearly the rationalist attitude of the Master whom Aquinas has in mind. That Master speaks as if he were a stranger to the Church. He regards as a necessary conclusion of reason something which contradicts the faith. And he

---

[3] See L. W. Keeler, *Sancti Thomae Aquinatis tractatus de unitate intellectus contra averroistas*, p. XII.

[4] *Ibid.*, pp. 78-80.

goes so far as to discuss in philosophy topics which belong strictly to sacred science. This attitude is much more radical and particularly more aggressive than that of Siger in the writings which have been found until the present time and which we are now going to consider. For these writings of Siger are the major *direct* witnesses of the rationalist tendency in the Arts Faculty before 1270.

As we have seen above, we have in our possession today two heterodox works of the Master from Brabant which are prior to the Condemnation of 1270: his *Quaestiones in tertium de anima*, and his *Quaestio utrum haec sit vera: "homo est animal", nullo homine existente*.[5] In these two writings Siger professes some positions which are clearly heretical: eternity of the world and of the human species; unicity of the human intellect; and as a consequence, denial of a future life for human individuals. He professes these heresies without any apparent concern for revealed truth. In fact, he closes his eyes to Christianity and thereby sidesteps any problem of reconciling faith and reason. Thus in his *Quaestiones in tertium de anima*, we have seen that when he discusses the temporal or eternal origin of the intellect, he does not oppose the solution of faith to that of reason, but rather that of Augustine to that of Aristotle, whom he favors. Farther on he takes up a question which he characterizes as "not very philosophical" (*non multum philosophica*), namely whether the soul when separated from the body can suffer from fire (a clear allusion to the fire of hell). He discusses and resolves this without wor-

---

[5] See above, pp. 6-8 and 35.

rying himself about contradicting Christian teaching. It must be noted, however, that one does not find in these writings, at least in the form in which they have come down to us, any attack against the faith, or any explicit profession of rationalism. The problem is simply ignored or at least passed over in silence.

Another direct witness to rationalist tendencies was examined by my late colleague and former student, Professor Maurice Giele, who died in 1966. This is the *Questions on Books I and II of the De anima*, a work by a Master who until now remains unknown. These *Questions* probably date from 1270. They are certainly after the *De unitate intellectus* of St. Thomas and probably before the Condemnation of December 10, 1270. The author holds to a radical Averroism, since he maintains that, properly speaking, man does not think. But here again the requirements of Christian orthodoxy are simply ignored. The unknown Master professes a *de facto* rationalism, without ever taking up the problem of the relationship between faith and reason.[6]

On December 10, 1270, Stephen Tempier, the Bishop of Paris, condemned thirteen propositions judged to be heretical. They correspond in large measure with the positions denounced by Bonaventure in his sermons of 1267 and 1268. Nonetheless, the episcopal decree does not speak of the rationalist attitude which is at the root of these errors.[7]

Such, then, are the direct and indirect indications we have today concerning the existence of a ratio-

---

[6] See F. Van Steenberghen, *Maître Siger de Brabant*, pp. 65-70.

[7] *Ibid.*, pp. 74-79.

nalist current of thought in the Faculty of Arts at Paris before 1270.

III

What was the reaction of Thomas Aquinas when he came face to face with this form of rationalism? It is to this question that I would like to respond in this part of the Lecture. It seems to me that his reaction was governed by certain broad principles, which I would now like to delineate.

The *first principle* Aquinas employed is the following. One must distinguish carefully between reason and faith, between philosophy and theology, between what can be demonstrated by reason and what can only be known by faith. Here are some illustrations of his concern for precision with respect to this.

One might begin with the very first question from his *Summa theologiae*, a question which deals with sacred doctrine (*De sacra doctrina*). There Thomas unfolds in clear terms the differences in object and in method which distinguish theology from the philosophical sciences. Siger of Brabant will be influenced by this question when he himself comes to distinguish in his turn between that "theology which is a part of philosophy" (what we today call natural theology) and that theology "which is called Sacred Scripture" (the science of revelation).[8]

As a second example one may turn to the controversy concerning the eternity of the world. As we saw in the First Lecture, on this issue Thomas always took the agnostic position. We can demonstrate by reason

---

[8] *Ibid.*, p. 225.

neither that the world is eternal nor that it began in time. Why did he adopt this position? He explains why in two passages already considered above in the First Lecture. He fears that if, while wishing to demonstrate by reason an article of faith, one has recourse to faulty argumentation, one will only elicit ridicule from unbelievers. Once more, then, one sees his concern to distinguish carefully between that which can be demonstrated by human reason and that which cannot. Boetius of Dacia, Siger's colleague, well understood Aquinas' attitude and made it his own.

A final example to illustrate Thomas' attitude may be found in the Prologue to his *De unitate intellectus.* There he explicitly states that he is going to deal with this question from a philosophical standpoint and not from that of faith. It is quite evident to everyone, he comments, that monopsychism contradicts the truth of Christian faith. But here we wish to show that it is incompatible with the principles of philosophy. Thomas was well aware that he would have to attack the Masters from the Arts Faculty on their own ground—that of philosophy.[9]

Thomas' *second principle* is this. Reason cannot contradict the faith. In other words, a truth established by reason cannot contradict one proposed by divine revelation for our belief. This principle is clearly stated in the final page of the *De unitate intellectus.* In citing the Master whose anti-Christian attitude he condemns, Aquinas writes: "What he then states is even more serious: 'By reason I necessarily conclude that the intellect is unique. But I firmly hold the op-

---

[9] L. W. Keeler, *Sancti Thomae . . de unitate intellectus*, p. 2, §2.

posite by faith.' He thinks, therefore, that faith has for its object affirmations whose contradictory can be established by necessary demonstration. But by necessary demonstration one can only arrive at that which is necessarily true, whose contradictory is false and impossible. It follows from his assertion that the faith has for its object that which is false and impossible, which even God cannot realize. The ears of the faithful cannot tolerate such language."

Thomas' second principle cannot be doubted by anyone who admits the divine origin of Christianity. Revealed truth cannot contradict rational truth. Yet the reconciliation of faith and reason has often proved difficult during the course of history. But that is due to human weaknesses since, on the one hand, it is often difficult to determine precisely the exact content of revelation and, on the other, it is just as difficult to know where the truth lies in the teachings proposed by the philosophers. Conflicts between faith and reason are always the result of misunderstandings which bear either upon what is true in terms of faith or on what is true according to reason. When Siger of Brabant defended as a philosophical truth the view that there is only one intellect for all mankind, he made a serious mistake with respect to philosophical truth. But when the Holy Office wanted to condemn the heliocentric theory defended by Galileo as contrary to Scripture, it was just as mistaken regarding revealed truth. A considerable amount of prudence is necessary whenever an apparent conflict arises between faith and reason.

A *third principle* which guided Aquinas' response to the rationalist position is this. The purpose of philosophy is not to know what previous philosophers have thought, but to grasp the real as it is. One finds a curious statement in Siger of Brabant's brief treatise, *De anima intellectiva*. There he declares that he is going to try to determine the thought of the philosophers more than to discover the truth, *since he is treating matters philosophically (cum philosophice procedamus)*.[10] At first sight this statement is shocking and almost incomprehensible, coming, as it does, from a professor of philosophy who is usually so anxious about the autonomy of philosophy. But one must remember that in the universities of the Middle Ages the essential role of a professor was to "read" (*legere*) the classical authors put on the program of studies by the Faculty. A course was known as a *lectio*, a term which is the root for the English "lecture." In the Faculty of Arts the Master's task was to "read," that is to say, to comment on the writings of Aristotle and other philosophers. Thus one can understand the frame of mind which Siger manifests in his surprising statement.

This understanding of philosophical investigation was reinforced for Siger and those like him by their extraordinary esteem for Aristotle, which led them more or less to identify "philosophy" with the "thought of Aristotle."

Thomas Aquinas, however, reacted strongly against this mentality in defending the third principle proposed above. He formulated it in a celebrated passage in his Commentary on the *De caelo et mundo*, which was one of his last writings, left unfinished at his

---

[10] B. Bazán, *Siger de Brabant. Quaestiones in tertium. . .* , p. 101: 6-9.

death. Near the end of Bk I of this Commentary he analyzes Aristotle's exposition of the different opinions of the Ancients concerning the origin of the cosmos. He observes in this regard that an examination of arguments advanced in support of opposing positions is very worthwhile for the discovery of the truth. But a little farther on, in noting the variety of interpretations of the ancient views on cosmogony, he states that we do not have to trouble ourselves too much with respect to these divergences, since philosophical inquiry does not have as its purpose to know what men have thought but what is the truth concerning reality. This is the third principle formulated above.[11]

I do not think that Thomas knew Siger's *De anima intellectiva*, where one finds the curious statement mentioned above. For Siger's treatise was composed in Paris ca. 1273 while Thomas was in Naples. In any event, we have no document indicating that Thomas was aware of it. Thus one cannot view the principle formulated by Thomas as a deliberate reply to Siger's statement. But this historical detail is not really important. What is much more important is the fact that the Dominican Master warns against servility to the philosophers. He knew well that the servility of Siger and his associates with respect to Aristotle was a fundamental cause of the intellectual crisis which they were undergoing and which had given birth to heterodox Aristotelianism. Under the guise of a rationalist concern for "freedom of thought" was hidden,

---

[11] See Thomas de Aquino, *In Aristotelis libros de caelo et mundo expositio*, liber I, lectio 22.

in fact, a philosophical dogmatism, an excessive cult for the Philosopher, a kind of philosophical "traditionalism."

Aquinas' *fourth guiding principle* in his response to rationalism is that divine revelation, through which we share in God's knowledge itself, is superior to human reason. It brings to reason valuable support and serves as its indispensable complement. This principle is developed especially in the first Question of the *Summa theologiae*. Revelation has a twofold object. On the one hand there are truths which are accessible to human reason, truths which God makes known to man in order to assist him in discovering them and to confirm him in their discovery. On the other hand, there are truths which are beyond human reason, the supernatural mysteries, that God reveals in order to make known his design concerning man's call to a supernatural life, a participation in the inner life of God himself.

An immediate corollary follows from this fourth principle. Provided that we are certain of the fact that such a doctrine is truly revealed, we must adhere to it firmly, no matter what contrary philosophical opinions there may be. Siger of Brabant perfectly understood this principle from 1270 and thereafter, and applied it many times in resolving his personal problems.

Such, then, is the general view on the relationship between reason and faith that Thomas Aquinas defended, and in terms of which he resisted the rationalist tendencies which had appeared in the Faculty of Arts.

IV

We could end our investigation at this point, since we have seen what was Thomas' attitude with respect to the rationalist tendencies in the Faculty of Arts. But it seems to me to be of interest to add some words concerning the influence his very firm and clear attitude had on Siger of Brabant. I shall speak of Siger because he is, until now, the only heterodox Master whose development after 1270 is well known to us, and on whom Thomas' influence is undeniable. This influence is already apparent in his *Questions on the Physics*, which date from 1270 or 1271. It is very evident in his *De anima intellectiva* and in his *Questions on the Metaphysics*, both ca. 1273. Finally, it is even more extensive and more pronounced in his last lectures as a Master, his *Quaestiones super librum de causis*, which date from ca. 1276. It is certain that Siger's esteem, even admiration, for Aquinas continued to grow after 1270. He uses Thomas' writings more and more extensively, although without naming him, in accord with the custom of that time. He refers to Albert the Great and Thomas as "most eminent men in philosophy" (*praecipui viri in philosophia*, *Albertus et Thomas*). But he maintains his independence and does not hesitate to criticize Thomas when he is in disagreement with him. In such cases he sometimes mentions Thomas by name (as in the *De anima intellectiva* and the *Questions on the Metaphysics*), but most frequently discusses his views without naming him.

Siger's appreciation for Thomas is not surprising if one bears in mind all that the two Masters had in common: their admiration for the work of Aristotle, the major source for their philosophy; their very clear views on the distinction between philosophical and theological knowledge, on the scientific autonomy of philosophy, and the distinctive character of its methods; their clear, lucid, and ordered thought; their predilection for metaphysics. Thomas' beneficial influence was undoubtedly decisive in Siger's return to orthodox ways, and this in turn gained for Siger clemency from the Curia's Tribunal where he had taken refuge in order to escape from the Inquisitor of France, Simon du Val.

Now let us consider more closely Siger's development after 1270. Thomas' intervention in his *De unitate intellectus* and Stephen Tempier's Condemnation of December 10, 1270, evidently opened the young Master's eyes. These events made him clearly aware of the moral and religious problem posed for him by his heterodox teaching. His writings after 1270 bear witness to his radical change in attitude, a change which was to increase during the following years.

From that time onward, whenever Siger is aware that he is exposing a position contrary to Christian dogma, he states that, in accord with his role as professor of philosophy, he is presenting the views of Aristotle or of other philosophers but without claiming that they are *true*. On the contrary, he lets us know that such positions are *erroneous* to the extent that they contradict the teachings of Christian revelation, which are always true. In his first writings after the Condemnation of 1270, he holds to this attitude.

But our philosopher comes to see more and more clearly that this position is not sufficient and therefore that it is not satisfying. For it limits itself to opposing certain philosophical conclusions to contrary

90

affirmations of the faith without explaining why such results of human reason are to be contested and rejected in the name of divinely revealed truth. Should philosophical investigation inevitably lead to erroneous conclusions? How can this be? Siger attempts to reply to these questions, as one can see in his *Questions on the Metaphysics* and his *De anima intellectiva*, where he tries to account for these antinomies between philosophy and the faith. Sometimes he attributes these divergencies to *supernatural* or *miraculous* interventions by God, which modify the normal course of nature. The prophets, as instruments of divine revelation, make us aware of the effects of these interventions which stem from divine freedom. Sometimes he stresses the weakness of human reason when faced with difficult metaphysical problems. Aristotle had compared the human intellect to the eyes of a night-bird which is blinded by the light of the sun. Sometimes he attempts to criticize, on philosophical grounds, conclusions from human science which contradict the faith. Time will not permit us to analyze all the passages where Siger attempts to account for the divergencies he sees between certain philosophical conclusions and certain truths of faith. These texts are of lively interest, both historical and psychological.

In his final lectures, his *Quaestiones super librum de causis*, Siger seems to have overcome his intellectual crisis. There he frequently affirms the superiority of the faith to reason. He does so calmly and in complete conformity with the principles of St. Thomas.

One might well wonder whether Siger's many professions of faith after 1270 are sincere or if they are simply intended to appease ecclesiastical authority and to avoid persecution from defenders of orthodoxy. Father P. Mandonnet, who had the merit of writing the first solid biography of Siger and who published some of his opuscula, proposed a very harsh interpretation of his thought and his religious attitude. Mandonnet did not believe in the sincerity of his professions of faith, and regarded him as a "free thinker" and a "rationalist" who concealed his heterodox convictions for reasons of prudence. He thought that, in order better to ward off suspicion, Siger had maintained the famous "double-truth" theory. According to this, a given thesis could be true in philosophy even though its contradictory thesis would be true according to faith and theology. Thus, for instance, according to philosophy the world is eternal in the past, while according to faith the world began to be.

Today, Mandonnet's views are completely dated. No historian now doubts Siger's sincerity. And it is certain that no Master in the Middle Ages defended the theory of double-truth, a position which is totally incompatible with the fundamental principles of Aristotelian philosophy.

Siger's sincerity is guaranteed by the psychological crisis he endured between 1270 and 1275, and by the efforts he made during this period to overcome the antinomies between faith and reason. If he had lost his faith, if he had become a "free-thinker," these attempts would have been senseless, and it would have been useless for him to go to so much trouble. It would have been enough for him to renew regularly his professions of faith while continuing to present the thought of the philosophers.[12]

It may be helpful for us to pause here to examine the theory of double-truth. Many historians continue to regard this as a characteristic teaching of the school which they refer to as "Latin Averroism." We are now familiar with the intellectual crisis of the thirteenth century, provoked as it was by the conflict between a Christian and a non-Christian view of the universe. In order to resolve this conflict and to appease defenders of orthodoxy, the "Averroists" would have adopted the double-truth theory. *A thesis can be true in philosophy* (for instance, eternity of the world in the past) and its *contradictory thesis can be true at the same time according to faith* (for instance, noneternity of the world in the past). Let us consider things more closely and attempt to determine precisely what was, in fact, the intellectual attitude of the Masters to whom the double-truth theory has been attributed.

Siger of Brabant

The first Christian Master to whom modern historians have imputed this theory is Siger of Brabant. We already know of his intellectual development after 1270 and his efforts to reconcile philosophy and the faith. His great historian, Mandonnet, turning to those texts which point to an inner crisis on the part of Siger and, after an analysis which is not unnu-

---

[12] On the evolution of Siger's attitude towards the faith after 1270 see Van Steenberghen, *Maître Siger de Brabant*, pp. 231-57.

anced, concludes in these terms: "One is not, therefore, justified in doubting as historical fact the contradictory position taken with respect to philosophy
and the faith by the Averroists in general and by Siger
of Brabant in particular."[13] Without speaking expressly of the theory of double-truth, in fact Mandonnet attributes this position to Siger. But the
expression "double-truth" had been in circulation
for a long time, and after Mandonnet's writings, it
was taken up, frequently in derivative publications
where, as usually happens, the reservations and nuances present in Mandonnet's work disappeared.

É. Gilson was the first to denounce as inexact the
formula "double-truth" for Siger of Brabant. In his
own examination of texts where Siger states his position concerning the antinomies between reason and
faith, this eminent historian establishes the following
facts: Siger never defends the compatibility of two
contradictory truths. In cases of conflict between philosophy and faith, Siger always states that the truth
is on the side of the faith.[14] One obviously may wonder whether these professions of faith are sincere,
continues Gilson, but that is another question. Mandonnet doubted Siger's sincerity and was inclined to
see in Averroism a "disguised form of free-think-
ing."[15] Gilson rather believes that Siger remained a

[13] P. Mandonnet, *Siger de Brabant et l'averroïsme latin au XIIIe siècle*,
1st ed. in Collectanea Friburgensia, VIII (Fribourg [Suisse], 1899), p.
CLXXI; 2nd ed. in Les Philosophes Belges VI-VII (Louvain, 1911-
1908), v. 1, pp. 152-53.

[14] É. Gilson, *Études de philosophie médiévale* (Strasbourg, 1921), p. 59:
"Ces philosophes n'enseignaient aucunement qu'il existe deux vérités
simultanées et contradictoires; Siger de Brabant déclare toujours que
la vérité est du côté de la foi."

[15] Mandonnet, *Siger de Brabant. . .* , 2nd ed., v. 1, p. 194.

convinced believer, and most recent historians have followed him, for reasons which I need not discuss here. In either case, the double-truth theory is excluded. If one follows Mandonnet, one makes of Siger a rationalist for whom truth is found on the side of reason. If one follows Gilson, truth falls on the side of faith. According to both, truth for Siger is one.

Boetius of Dacia

Let us now consider Boetius of Dacia, a colleague of Siger in the Faculty of Arts at Paris. Controversies concerning Siger of Brabant had led to almost unanimous agreement in support of Gilson's views. Even if one hesitated to recognize Siger's sincerity, there was no longer any question of imputing to him the double-truth theory. The choice was rather between Siger the "rationalist" and Siger the "fideist." This was the situation when the Hungarian scholar, G. Sajó, then librarian for manuscripts in the National Library of Budapest, thought he had discovered a real defender of the double-truth theory in the person of Boetius of Dacia. After recalling that, according to Gilson, "the double-truth theory had never been sustained," and that this opinion had been supported by many historians, Sajó continues: "The discovery of the *De mundi aeternitate* of Boetius of Dacia renders these recent suppositions untenable." In his subsequent interpretation of Boetius' position, Sajó thinks that the double-truth theory implies, for this Master, a relativistic notion of truth, which is devoid of any absolute validity. Revealed truth and philosophical truth are truths *secundum quid*, "that is to say, relative to the premises from which they are drawn."[16]

F. Sassen, the well known Dutch medievalist, who has been interested in Siger and his school for a long time, accepted Sajó's views without reservation. He believed that one can account for this relativistic understanding of truth because of the excessive influence of sophistical exercises in the Faculty of Arts. From this there would have resulted an exaggerated attention to the purely formal value of argumentation without sufficient concern for the content and real value of the premises.[17]

One can imagine my curiosity when I turned to the text of Boetius' opusculum after having taken note of Sajó's and Sassen's commentaries. If their interpretation was accurate, one would now have discovered a Master who, while belonging to Siger's group, would have defended a position on the relation between faith and reason which differed profoundly from his. It would moreover be necessary to admit, against every likelihood, that in the midst of the thirteenth century, an Aristotelian philosopher defended the compatibility of two contradictory truths.

My personal examination of this opusculum proved to be quite surprising. Not only does Boetius not teach the double-truth theory, but his fundamental thesis and the main purpose of his exposition is to show that there is *no real disagreement*, no real contradiction, between the findings of philosophy and the

---

[16] G. Sajó, *Un traité récemment découvert de Boèce de Dacie De mundi aeternitate* (Budapest, 1954), pp. 36-37 and 71-74.

[17] F. Sassen, "Boëthius van Dacie en de theorie van de dubbele waarheid," *Studia catholica* 30 (1955), pp. 262-73.

faith (*[philosophorum] sententia in nullo contradicit sententiae christianae fidei nisi apud non intelligentes*).[18] The same point is clearly stated at the end of the work (*Ideo nulla est contradictio inter fidem et Philosophum*).[19] In order to illustrate the justification for his position, Boetius takes as his example the problem of the world's duration in the past. What, he asks, is philosophy's position on this matter? No philosophical science (neither physics, nor mathematics, nor metaphysics) can, starting from its own principles, demonstrate that the world began to be. On the other hand, none of these sciences can demonstrate the eternity of the world. In sum, then, before this question philosophy is agnostic and, as a consequence, there is not even the appearance of a conflict with the faith, according to which the world began to exist. The reason for philosophy's inability to resolve this question is the fact that the duration of the universe depends on God's free will. But we can only know what God has willed when he deigns to reveal this to us.[20]

---

[18] Sajó, *Un traité . . .*, p. 83:21-23.

[19] *Ibid.*, p. 118: 962-963.

[20] *Ibid.*, pp. 84-117. Boetius' opusculum is fascinating from beginning to end. For an analysis of this as well as for a critique of Sajó's and Sassen's interpretations see Van Steenberghen, "Nouvelles recherches sur Siger de Brabant et son école," *Revue philosophique de Louvain* 54 (1956), pp. 137-47. Also see Van Steenberghen, *La philosophie au XIIIe siècle*, pp. 404-11. Sajó has acknowledged his mistake in a communication to the International Congress at Cologne in 1961: "Boetius de Dacia und seine philosophische Bedeutung," in the Acts of the Congress, *Die Metaphysik im Mittelalter*, Miscellanea mediaevalia, 2 (Berlin, 1963), pp. 454-63. He has reedited Boetius' opusculum on the basis of five manuscripts, resulting in a greatly superior text to that of the first edition. See *Boetii de Dacia tractatus de aeternitate mundi. Editio altera*, Quellen und Studien zur Geschichte der Philosophie IV (Berlin, 1964).

As one will note, Boetius' views with respect to the problem of the world's eternity coincide with those of Thomas Aquinas. One could discuss them, and, for my part, I would only accept them partially. But in any event they are perfectly orthodox and are in no way connected with the double-truth theory.

One may wonder how it was possible for the editor of Boetius' treatise to have misunderstood so completely the author's intentions and the meaning of his exposition. A librarian by profession, Sajó is neither a philosopher nor an historian of philosophy. He was not sufficiently prepared for the work of interpretation which he undertook. One sees this when he takes up his examination of the treatise's teaching, since he proposes the following definition of the double-truth theory: "According to this, two opposed truths, namely, one that is theological and another that is philosophical, could be valid at the same time (*simul stare possunt*), *without contradicting one another*."[21] It is clear that this definition is completely unacceptable, since it attributes to eventual defenders of the double-truth theory an even more flagrant incoherence than that normally ascribed to them. For one now assigns to them a contradiction in terms in the strict sense, since two opposed (contradictory) truths would not contradict one another. Never was such an enormity defended by any medieval Master, and there is no trace of this in Boetius' *De mundi aeternitate*. The problem for Siger and his contemporaries is to determine what one should think and do when philosophical investigation leads to a con-

---

[21] Sajó, *Un traité* . . . , p. 35. Italics mine. The author gives an interesting bibliography on the double-truth question.

clusion which *contradicts* a certain affirmation of Christian revelation, for instance, when philosophy concludes that the world is eternal, while Christian doctrine maintains that the world is not eternal. Here one is indeed dealing with *contradictory* propositions, and the double-truth theory would consist in holding that two contradictory propositions can both be true at one and the same time.

Having started from this faulty notion, Sajó inevitably had to go astray. He seems to have been misled likewise by certain expressions which are, at first sight, shocking, as when Boetius affirms that the physicist (natural philosopher) should *deny* truths which contradict his principles and destroy his science, such as the resurrection of the dead, or the instantaneous cure of a man born blind. But Boetius explains that he should deny these truths *from the particular point of view* of his science and its principles, even though he admits them and believes them to be possible through the intervention of a Cause superior to natural causes. Scientific truths are true under a certain respect (*secundum quid*), that is to say, within the limits of the principles and methods of natural science, while truth revealed by God has an absolute value (*veritas simpliciter*).

Ferrand of Spain

A. Zimmermann, President of the Thomas-Institut of the University of Cologne, has recently made known a Spanish commentator on Aristotle's *Metaphysics*, Ferrand of Spain.[22] His Commentary, which

---

[22] A. Zimmermann, "Ein Averroist des späten 13. Jahrhunderts: Ferrandus de Hispania," *Archiv für Geschichte der Philosophie* 50 (1968), pp. 145-64.

was probably composed ca. 1290, deals with Bks I-III, VI-X, and XII of Aristotle's text. In his work of exegesis he expressly takes as his guide Averroes, whom he regards as the best interpreter of Aristotle. This assessment is due, one may suppose, to his study of the texts, but he acknowledges in artless fashion that his sympathy for the Philosopher from Córdoba can perhaps also be explained by the fact that he himself was born in that same region. Now, he explains, proximity in place is one of the causes for similarity in natures, as Aristotle teaches. He adds, however, that his great esteem for Averroes' work as a commentator in no way diminishes his respect for the truth whatever it may be.

Zimmermann notes that Ferrand distinguishes sharply between the problem of interpreting Aristotle's texts and that of the truth of his teaching. He also points out passages where Ferrand asserts his unconditioned attachment to the truth of the Catholic faith or *to any other truth*, even if it happens that Aristotle teaches the opposite. On the other hand, however, when it comes to the doctrine of creation, Zimmermann suspects that Ferrand's intentions may not be completely pure. For while declaring that truth is to be found on the side of faith, he lets it be understood that the contrary views of Aristotle are not all that inaccurate and that they are acceptable on the level of philosophy of nature. And Zimmermann continues in these terms: "In reading these passages one has the impression, not without reason, that Ferrand's remarks are rather intended to avoid the known reproach of defending the doctrine of double-truth, as victims of the Condemnation of 1277 were

accustomed to do. As to whether Ferrand unequiv-
ocally professed this position, this cannot be settled
until one has studied his entire work." Finally, at
the end of his study, the author concludes that Ferrand is "an Averroist in the strict meaning of the
term," that is to say, an authentic disciple of Averroes and hence, a precursor of John of Jandun, who
boasted of being the "ape" of Aristotle and his Arab
Commentator.

I do not agree with these views of Zimmermann
about Ferrand of Spain. We know today of learned
interpreters of Aristotle who nonetheless do not pro-
fess Aristotelian philosophy. Among them there are
some who hold Averroes' Commentaries in great esteem and judge them to be more faithful to the Philosopher's thought than those of Aquinas or than the
paraphrases of Albert the Great. But no one would
dream of regarding these commentators as "Averroists." The question therefore arises: Does one find
in the Middle Ages certain commentators who are
only commentators, commentators on Aristotle who
regularly rely on Averroes, but who limit themselves
in this to their role as exegetes without adopting the
doctrines which they explain? Ferrand of Spain seems
to be an excellent example of this. He interprets Aristotle's text with the assistance of Averroes' commentary, without ever committing himself as to his
own thought and even while clearly distancing himself from the Philosopher and his Commentator. In
the conclusion to his commentary he explicitly distinguishes the search for truth from the exegete's task.
He rejects every human authority and every human
argument which contradicts the truth of Christian

faith. On the other side, his commentary does not betray any trace of an intellectual crisis nor any anxiety, but exudes serenity and sincerity. In brief, all happens there as if, having learned from Siger's disappointments and from the Parisian crisis of 1267-1277, the Spanish Master deliberately limited himself to the role of historian of doctrines. And when he departs from this role, it is in order to address certain criticisms to the Philosopher or the Commentator in the name of revealed truth and, sometimes, even in the name of right reason. The facts being such, there is clearly no place for the double-truth theory in Ferrand's intellectual attitude.

John of Jandun

With John of Jandun we come to the fourteenth century. According to B. Geyer, this Parisian Master, who taught in the Faculty of Arts around 1310, clearly professed the double-truth theory.[23] At first sight, this would not seem to be unreasonable. "It seems to us," writes Sassen, "that the double-truth theory is not possible until that moment when, among Averroists in the fourteenth century, it is grounded on the voluntarist position according to which God can render possible that which is impossible. Consequently, two contradictory propositions could both be true at the same time."[24] I wrote in similar terms in 1942: ". . . such a doctrine, conceivable perhaps

---

[23] B. Geyer, *Fr. Ueberwegs Grundriss der Geschichte der Philosophie. Zweiter Teil, Die patristische und scholastische Philosophie*, 11th ed. (Berlin, 1928), p. 616.

[24] F. Sassen, "Siger de Brabant et la doctrine de la double vérité," *Revue Néoscolastique de Philosophie* 33 (1931), p. 179.

within the nominalist climate of the fourteenth century, is completely incompatible with Siger's epistemology and with his way of understanding divine power."[25] This was to suppose that within the skeptical and relativistic atmosphere which was widespread in the fourteenth century, a Master could have taught the doctrine of the double-truth without immediately provoking thereby universal reprobation from all of his colleagues.

But in fact Jandun's philosophical work dates from the beginning of the century, at a time when the critical and skeptical tendencies had scarcely begun to appear. And examination of the texts of this Averroist Master reveals an attitude that conforms, in its essentials, to that of his predecessors in the thirteenth century. When faced with an antinomy between philosophy and Christian teaching, he regularly states that the truth is found on the side of faith. There is never any question of two contradictory truths. But one can detect a considerable difference between the personal dispositions of Jandun and those of Siger. While, at least after 1270, Siger attempts to find some explanation for the divergences that he perceives between certain philosophical conclusions and religious teachings, Jandun parades without shame the oppositions which he believes exist and states that he is incapable of overcoming them.

This admission of his inability to resolve these antinomies seems to betray some annoyance on his part as well as his refusal to attempt to reconcile faith and

---

[25] F. Van Steenberghen, *Siger de Brabant d'après ses oeuvres inédites. II. Siger dans l'histoire de l'aristotélisme*, in Les Philosophes Belges XIII (Louvain, 1942), p. 688.

reason. This bad humor in one who is also known as a declared adversary of the papacy has led most historians to cast doubt on the sincerity of his professions of faith. Jandun would be, in fact, a rationalist, a free-thinker. He would conceal his hand in order to avoid any difficulty with defenders of orthodoxy.

Nonetheless, these apparently judicious conclusions have been challenged by one of Jandun's most recent historians. At the end of a detailed and well documented study, S. MacClintock concludes that this lack of belief on the part of the Averroist Master has never been demonstrated.[26] This judgment rejoins that offered by A. Maier in her research concerning the double-truth theory among the major Masters in Arts in the fourteenth century, John Buridan and Nicholas Oresme. According to her, no scholastic ever defended the existence of two contradictory truths. All maintain that the absolute truth is to be found on the side of divine revelation and in most cases we have no serious reason to doubt their sincerity. The rationalist attitude appears only toward the end of the fourteenth century, with men such as Blaise of Parma. This attitude heralds the approach of the Renaissance.[27]

---

[26] S. MacClintock, *Perversity and Error. Studies on the "Averroist" John of Jandun* (Indiana University: Bloomington, 1956). The fourth part of this work is entitled: "Faith, Reason, and the Double Truth" (pp. 69-101). The author states that he began his study of the Parisian Master with the usual prejudices relating to his Averroism, his duplicity, and his unbelief. Examination of his texts has forced him to revise or at least to reserve his judgment.

[27] A. Maier, *Metaphysische Hintergründe der spätscholastischen Naturphilosophie*, in *Studien zur Naturphilosophie der Spätscholastik* IV (Rome, 1955), ch. 1.

Rationalism

Averroes

What is one to say of Averroes himself. Did he originate the double-truth theory? Considerable study has been devoted to the Philosopher from Córdoba's attitude vis-à-vis the Koran and the Muslim religion. It is not certain that his attitude was always the same. What is certain is that he never proposed a doctrine which bears any resemblance to the double-truth theory. He maintains, one may suppose, that the Koran, being of divine origin, is addressed to all classes of minds and that it should be interpreted differently by the simple believer, by the theologian, and by the philosopher. But these interpretations are not equally true. The first two are only approximations and are "true" to the extent that they can be reduced to the third, which alone is absolutely true. Averroes' respect for the Koran conceals, therefore, a decidedly rationalist option. Reason judges in the final analysis and it is reason that determines the authentic meaning to be given to the sacred text. There is only one truth for Averroes, therefore, that of the philosophers.[28]

An Obstinate Legend and Its Origins

Let us here bring our investigation to a close. It has not been exhaustive, for I have not drawn upon many anonymous documents which are part of the literature of heterodox Aristotelianism or of Latin Averroism. Nor have I examined here the Italian Aver-

---

[28] On Averroes' attitude vis-à-vis the Muslim religion see E. Renan, *Averroès et l'averroïsme*, Première partie, fourth edition (Paris, 1882); L. Gauthier, *La théorie d'Ibn Rochd (Averroès) sur les rapports de la religion et de la philosophie* (Paris, 1909); and *Ibn Rochd (Averroès)*, Les grands philosophes (Paris, 1948).

roists of the fourteenth and fifteenth centuries. But I can assure the reader that these witnesses, passed over here so as not to prolong unduly my exposition, contribute nothing new to the solution of the problem under examination.

The first and most important conclusion which follows from our investigation is this: *No one in the Middle Ages defended the double-truth theory.* No one maintained that two contradictory propositions can both be true at the same time. This historical fact, guaranteed by all of the sources at our disposal, was foreseeable. How could one imagine that thinkers so imbued with Aristotelian teachings, so intensively trained in dialectic, and so filled with admiration for the Stagirite, could have disregarded so completely that logical law which is for Aristotle "the first principle": the principle of non-contradiction? As regards Siger of Brabant, his teaching on this point is as explicit and as firm as one could wish. Article VI of his *Impossibilia* is a discussion with a "Sophist" who casts doubt on this "first principle." Siger replies that this principle is absolutely necessary, that its denial is unthinkable, and that no one can be convinced at the same time of two statements which explicitly contradict one another. Elsewhere, in replying to an argument of Thomas Aquinas, Siger states that God himself in his omnipotence cannot do that which implies contradiction.[29] Thus J. P. Müller could write: "One cannot fail to note the insistence, one might even say the em-

---

[29] *De anima intellectiva*, ch. 7. See Bazán, *Siger de Brabant. Quaestiones in tertium de anima. De anima intellectiva. De aeternitate mundi*, p. 103: 49-50. For Art. VI of the *Impossibilia* see Bazán, *Siger de Brabant. Écrits de logique, de morale et de physique*, pp. 92-97.

phasis, with which Siger removes any foundation for the double-truth thesis."[30] All Aristotelians in the Middle Age speak in the same way. I know of no exception.

But, then, how account for this mistake on the part of so many historians? They surely did not dream up the double-truth theory. The *double-truth theory has resulted from a superficial and incorrect interpretation of two sets of texts*: those which express the position of heterodox Masters, and those which contain their opponents' reaction. Such will be our second conclusion, but it calls for a brief justifying commentary.

The heterodox Masters are responsible for the celebrated theory because of the blunt way in which they often oppose philosophical conclusions and statements of Christian teaching. Thus one of them demonstrates, following Aristotle, that the world and motion are eternal in the past. Then he immediately adds: "But according to faith the world has begun and movement has begun. And this should not be demonstrated, for if it were demonstrable, faith would be superfluous." Or again: "It is true that, according to faith, many immaterial forms can exist in the same species. But according to Aristotle and all the philosophers, this is impossible." The authors of such statements indeed add that the truth is found on the side of faith. But one *has the impression* that they remain attached to the conclusions of philosophy, and that, without admitting this expressly, they

---

[30] J. P. Müller, "Philosophie et foi chez Siger de Brabant. La théorie de la double vérité," in *Miscellanea philosophica R. P. Josepho Gredt, O.S.B. completis LXXV annis oblata*, Studia Anselmiana 7-8 (Rome, 1938), p. 40.

hold as true two contradictory propositions. *In fact*, they feel that they are driven to a choice which is very painful for them, and which many of them cannot bring themselves to make. This accounts for the persisting malaise that one finds in Siger of Brabant.

On the other hand, defenders of orthodoxy quickly recognized this confusion on the part of these Christian followers of Aristotle. This is indicated by the concluding page of Thomas' *De unitate intellectus* wherein he denounces Siger's equivocal attitude, and which we have already cited above. There Thomas rebukes him for holding that "faith has for its object affirmations whose contradictory can be established by necessary demonstration." From this it will follow that the faith has for its object "that which is false and impossible, that which even God cannot realize."[31] Stephen Tempier, the Bishop of Paris, speaks in a similar vein in the prologue to his famed Condemnation of 219 propositions in 1277: "In order not to appear to support the theses which they expose, they camouflage their solutions. They say, in effect, that these are true according to philosophy, but not according to Catholic faith, as if there were two contrary truths."[32]

---

[31] Keeler, *Sancti Thomae . . . de unitate intellectus*, p. 79. Also see above, p. 53. Thomas does not attribute to Siger the double-truth theory. He rather forces him to say that the faith teaches doctrines that are "false and impossible."

[32] *Chartularium Universitatis Parisiensis*, T. I, p. 543. Also in Mandonnet, *Siger* . . . , 2nd ed., v. 2, p. 175. "Ne autem quod sic innuunt asserere videantur, responsiones ita palliant quod, dum cupiunt vitare Scillam, incidunt in Charibdim. Dicunt enim ea esse vera secundum philosophiam, sed non secundum fidem catholicam, quasi sint duae contrariae veritates." The *quasi* should be noted. Here again, Tempier does not say that the condemned Masters affirm the existence of a double-truth.

As one can see, opponents of the heterodox Masters wanted to force them into the double-truth theory, in order to show that their position was absolutely untenable. This leads us to formulate one final conclusion. The double-truth theory is a clumsy and inaccurate expression used by many modern historians to characterize an *intellectual crisis* created for a certain number of thinkers, beginning in the thirteenth century, by the meeting between non-Christian philosophy and Christian thought. This crisis was an especially grave episode in the troubled history of the relationships between faith and reason, between religious thought and rational knowledge.[33]

CONCLUSION

From this Third Lecture, we may draw two conclusions, one historical and one religious.

On the historical side, it is clear that there were rationalist tendencies in the Faculty of Arts at Paris between 1265 and 1270. But this rationalist thrust seems to have been largely contained after 1270. Thomas Aquinas contributed effectively to its neutralization. This is certainly true in the case of Siger of Brabant, and it seems that one may draw the same conclusion with respect to Boetius of Dacia. The Condemnation of 1277 was often unjust to the two leaders of this movement, Siger and Boetius, as regards many of the 219 articles which were proscribed.[34]

---

[33] For fuller discussion of the double-truth theory see Van Steenberghen, *Introduction à l'étude de la philosophie médiévale*, Philosophes médiévaux XVIII (Louvain-Paris, 1974), pp. 555-70.

[34] See R. Hissette, *Enquête sur les 219 articles condamnés à Paris le 7 mars 1277*, Philosophes médiévaux XXII (Louvain-Paris, 1977).

On the religious side, history leaves for us a lesson in both prudence and modesty. In a case of apparent conflict between a scientific thesis and a religious doctrine, one must investigate very carefully and with an exacting critical sense in order to determine whether the scientific thesis is solidly established and whether the religious doctrine is really contained in the deposit of revelation. Such investigation will always result in dispelling misunderstandings and in showing that the conflict was more apparent than real.

INDEX OF NAMES

111

INDEX OF TOPICS